AQUA
2003

AQUARIUS
2003

Jane Struthers

p

This is a Parragon Book
First published in 2002

Parragon
Queen Street House
4 Queen Street
Bath BA1 1HE
UK

Produced by Magpie Books, an imprint of
Constable & Robinson Ltd, London

Illustrations courtesy of Slatter-Anderson, London
Cover courtesy of Simon Levy

ISBN 0-75258-669-6

A copy of the British Library Cataloguing-in-Publication Data
is available from the British Library

Printed and bound in the EC

CONTENTS

Dates for 2003

Aquarius 21 January – 18 February

Pisces 19 February – 20 March

Aries 21 March – 20 April

Taurus 21 April – 21 May

Gemini 22 May – 21 June

Cancer 22 June – 22 July

Leo 23 July – 23 August

Virgo 24 August – 23 September

Libra 24 September – 23 October

Scorpio 24 October – 22 November

Sagittarius 23 November – 21 December

Capricorn 22 December – 20 January

INTRODUCTION

Dear Aquarius

Happy 2003! I hope you have a fantastic year with the aid of this book. It's designed to help you make the most of the highlights and steer yourself quickly through the low points.

If you can't wait to find out what 2003 holds for you, turn immediately to **The Year 2003**, my summary of what you can expect in your relationships, health, money and career. My day by day forecasts for 2003 follow on, with at-a-glance charts that give you the general flavour of each month.

Your Aquarius Sun Sign is full of information about what makes you tick, and particularly about how you operate in four areas of your life: relationships, health, money and career. If you've recently met someone new and you want to know whether your signs hit it off, turn to **Love and the Stars** to find out what astrology says about your relationship. It's a quick guide to your compatibility with each of the twelve signs, and is followed by two charts that show how you get on with the other signs in love and sex, and also in friendship.

Speaking of friendship, how important are friends to you? **Family and Friends** will give you the answers and also reveal what you really think about your family. Do you simply tolerate them or are they the centre of your world?

If you've never been sure whether you're Capricorn, Aquarius or Pisces because you were born at the start or end of Aquarius, **Born on the Cusp?** will solve the problem once and for all.

Once you've read all that you'll be thoroughly equipped for 2003, so enjoy it!

Jane Struthers

THE YEAR 2003

 Friends and Lovers

There's good news for your relationships this year because they look all set to flourish in many different ways. One-to-one relationships will be very enjoyable and satisfying between January and late August, and on the whole during this time you'll be much happier with other people than when you're by yourself. It's a fantastic period for any sort of team work, whether you're doing it for personal or business reasons, because you'll really want your alliances to work well. If you're currently a solo Aquarian, you might soon have someone new on your arm, especially if your relationship is a whirlwind romance.

Close relationships benefit from late September onwards, giving you the chance to establish a greater sense of intimacy with some of the people in your life. You might want to do this sexually or you may prefer to forge strong emotional links with someone.

If you're involved in a love affair as 2003 starts, don't be surprised if it seems a little low-key or not as exciting as you'd like. What you lose in excitement you might gain in emotional satisfaction, and also in a tremendous understanding of each other. However, any shaky or unhappy alliances could fall by the wayside now unless you're really prepared to work at them and try to heal them.

Don't underestimate the effect that friends have on you throughout the year. They may encourage you to think deeply about something or may even introduce you to a completely new way of life.

Health

During the past few years you've been subject to strange fluctuations in your energy levels. Sometimes you've felt completely energized and lively, and on other occasions it's almost as though someone has pulled out the plug and all your vitality has drained away. This situation will continue in 2003, encouraging you to take extra care of your health and to ensure you catch up on lost sleep or skipped meals whenever you get the chance. You might become interested in a complementary therapy in 2003 because you'll be drawn to ideas that aren't conventional. However, don't neglect traditional medicine if it has something to offer you or is the obvious answer to your problems. You don't want to take any risks with your health!

From early June it's even more important than usual that you take care of yourself because you'll be kept very busy in other areas of your life. If you feel tired, make sure you get plenty of rest. It will be quite easy to burn yourself out without really noticing it. Keep an eye on the condition of your skin, teeth and nails because these could all indicate that you need to take more care of yourself. You should also take extra care of your bones during this time.

Money

In 2003 you'll start to see changes to the state of your finances. These changes will continue to affect you for the next few years and in 2003 you may only get a brief flavour of what's to come. So what should you expect? Well, the state of your finances may be quite erratic during the next few years, with periods of feast followed by periods of famine. Your spending patterns may reflect this, so sometimes you'll want to buy almost everything within reach and at other periods you'll prefer to save your money. If you are thinking of investing your cash, consider buying technological items such as computers, televisions and other pieces of electronic wizardry.

Ideally, you should try to save regular sums of money in case you need them for a rainy day. There will be a certain amount of unpredictability in your finances during the next few years so it's a wise move to make allowances for this. Although you may fancy experimenting with some unusual or brand-new savings accounts, make sure you know what you're doing.

There's good news from late August onwards because you could receive an unexpected windfall or pay-out. For instance, you might discover that you qualify for a tax rebate or you might get a lump sum from an endowment policy. If you're lucky, you might also benefit from a partner's generosity.

Career

Make the most of your creativity between the start of 2003 and early June. You'll enjoy converting your ideas into reality and creating something concrete out of your inspiring thoughts. If you're hoping to make your name through an artistic project or job, give it all you've got now and see what happens. Things may develop rather slowly, so don't expect overnight success, but they could build into something wonderful and highly satisfying.

The picture changes from early June, when you enter a two-year phase in which work will keep you very busy. There may even be periods when you'll be rushed off your feet and have to put in some overtime in order to get everything done in time. However, try to make these phases of overwork the exception rather than the rule – otherwise you'll find that you've set a precedent that will gradually erode your spare time. You'll start to feel exhausted and you might also be resentful about having to work such long hours. Nevertheless, the work you do during this time will be valuable, especially if it involves providing a service or helping people in need.

If you're hoping to introduce some dramatic or radical changes to your working life, try to complete as many of them as possible this year while your prospects are still so favourable. What happens in mid-May could be highly significant, telling you whether you're on the right track or you need to make some more adjustments. You may also have to take other people's needs and fears into account, especially if you're making decisions that will ultimately affect their quality of life. So be prepared to talk things through and to find compromises rather than to insist on having everything your own way.

Your Day by Day Guide

JANUARY AT A GLANCE

Love	❤ ❤ ❤ ❤ ❤
Money	£ $
Career	💻 💻 💻
Health	☼ ☼ ☼ ☼ ☼

• *Wednesday 1 January* •

You greet 2003 with a sense of optimism and excitement, even if you did stay up too late last night. You aren't concerned with mundane trifles like that because you're so keen to do something memorable or interesting now. If you want to start the year as you mean to go on, get together with people who always make you think and who remind you that life has so much to offer.

• *Thursday 2 January* •

Right on cue, today's New Moon will give you a lot of pep during the coming fortnight. It will also remind you to get cracking on any projects or tasks that have slipped your mind or which you've been putting off because you don't like the look of them. You might get involved in something behind the scenes, too, such as a cloak-and-dagger assignation with someone.

• *Friday 3 January* •

If anyone tries to restrict your options or limit your movements today, you'll soon see red. You will also want to make it clear in no uncertain terms that you aren't prepared to put up with such limitations and constraints, and if necessary you'll be quite vociferous about this. Alternatively, if you're the one trying to lay down the law to a certain person, you'll have to be prepared for them to react very strongly and unfavourably to what you are suggesting. Tricky.

• Saturday 4 January •

Try to take things easy whenever you get the chance today because you don't have as much energy and stamina as usual. You may even feel quite defeated and miserable if things don't go your way. Do yourself a favour and try to steer clear of any situations or people that you find stressful because they will be even harder to cope with than usual now. Instead, you need some peace and quiet.

• Sunday 5 January •

If you're worried about something, it will help to confide in someone you trust today. You will find it much easier to open up than you expected, and it will be a great relief to be able to pour out your heart to a sympathetic listener. If you don't know anyone who fits the bill, consider ringing a suitable telephone helpline because they could help to set your mind at rest.

• Monday 6 January •

The emotional stakes are raised today, leading to a lot of hot air and some slightly overblown scenes. For instance, you may take things too much to heart or get rather agitated about them, even if you would usually shrug them off. Or you might have to deal with someone who's making a big fuss about something and who won't be happy until they've got everyone's attention.

• *Tuesday 7 January* •

Friends are a real joy to be with between now and early February. You'll love getting together with them whenever you have the chance, particularly if they're providing some light relief from whatever else is going on in your life at the moment. There is also a chance that someone who starts as a chum will soon occupy a more important place in your heart, especially if you're single at the moment.

• *Wednesday 8 January* •

Your financial situation could easily get you down today. You may open a bill and freeze with horror, or you might tot up everything you spent in December and wonder how on earth you're going to manage. This is a good day for making some practical decisions, so try to rise above any sense of panic and deal with the facts. It will be reassuring to know that you're doing something constructive.

• *Thursday 9 January* •

You've got a real drive to get ahead today, and you'll enjoy getting on with whatever needs to be tackled. Ideally, you should do all this by yourself and without anyone else around, because that will be the best way to be productive now. This is also a good day for thinking things through by yourself because you could reach some important decisions that you will feel proud of.

• *Friday 10 January* •

Oh dear! It's one of those days when you seem to be tiptoeing through a minefield of problems, with various people apparently eager to jump down your throat at the slightest opportunity. You may also have a hair-trigger temper now, especially if someone mentions something that you were hoping to keep secret or are desperately trying not to think about.

• *Saturday 11 January* •

It seems that there are certain things you need to get off your chest, either by confiding in someone sympathetic or by pouring out your heart into your diary or journal. You certainly can't bottle things up for much longer and you'll feel so much better when you've expressed your angst. Although things may be tough at the moment, spare a thought for other people who are also going through hard times.

• *Sunday 12 January* •

You more than live up to your Aquarian reputation for being independent today, because you'll stage a rebellion at the merest hint of anyone trying to restrict you or clip your wings. You won't take kindly to any unnecessary rules or regulations that are foisted on you, either, and it seems that you aren't prepared to entertain any give or take about this. Once you put your foot down you will be immovable.

• *Monday 13 January* •

You're in a much more reasonable mood today, and may even wonder why you got so worked up yesterday. This is a lovely day to surround yourself with your creature comforts and also with some of your nearest and dearest. If you're thinking about making some home improvements, start making plans now even if you aren't yet ready to put them into practice. Let them percolate through your mind first.

• *Tuesday 14 January* •

A certain person craves attention today and they won't be happy until they've got it. They could cause a bit of a fuss if they think they're being neglected or they might get involved in a spot of rivalry. Try to play this down to avoid the situation becoming overblown. If you need some light relief, immerse yourself in one of your favourite hobbies or take yourself off to a club or the pub.

• *Wednesday 15 January* •

There's a slight chill between you and a loved one today. What's it all about and is it a cause for worry? With luck, it will all blow over very soon although it may not be very pleasant in the meantime. For instance, a special person may be rather distant with you or they might not have time for you. If you were looking forward to a social event, it could be postponed or even cancelled, much to your disappointment.

• *Thursday 16 January* •

You're in a much more sparky mood than you were yesterday, and as a result you're keen to do something enjoyable or unusual. How about visiting a restaurant or bar that you've never tried before, or going to the cinema to see one of the latest releases? There could be a surprise with a loved one, perhaps when they reveal a new side to their character. You will be intrigued!

• *Friday 17 January* •

Friends make you feel cherished today, so try to meet up with some chums even if it's only for a quick drink. You'll be touched by the concern that a friend shows you, and they may even offer to do you a favour that's above and beyond the call of duty. You also have the milk of human kindness flowing through your veins right now, and may want to contribute your time or money to a philanthropic cause.

• Saturday 18 January •

There's a Full Moon today and it's urging you to sort out any problems connected with your health or work. If you've been struggling with a persistent ailment or symptom, get some medical advice about it during the coming fortnight. If you're fed up with your current job or are unhappy with some of your working conditions, use this time to see what you can do to improve the situation.

• Sunday 19 January •

It's almost impossible to pin down a certain person today. They're being very slippery, and there's even a chance that you may fail to make contact with them at all. Think twice before entering any form of agreement with someone today because you may not be in complete possession of the facts. You may also be prepared to put up with things that you would normally find totally unacceptable.

• Monday 20 January •

The tenor of your life changes from today, and during the next four weeks you'll be blessed with extra energy and confidence. This will be a super opportunity to push ahead with projects that you've been meaning to tackle for ages, and it's also a great chance to start turning some of your New Year resolutions into reality. So set yourself some tasks and see how many you have ticked off by this time next month.

• *Tuesday 21 January* •

This promises to be a fabulous day, full of laughter, enjoyment and conviviality. It's a super day for taking part in any sort of social event because you're bound to have a good time. If you're reading this in advance and are wondering when to have your birthday party, this is a fabulous day for a celebration. There will also be a wonderful rapport between you and a certain someone.

• *Wednesday 22 January* •

A close relationship goes through the doldrums today. This will make you feel low-key and miserable unless you can manage to rise above it. Do your best not to brood about things or feel too sorry for yourself. Instead, try to find productive ways to remedy the current problems or distract yourself by doing something that you always enjoy.

• *Thursday 23 January* •

A positive attitude brings some fabulous results today, so keep smiling whenever possible. You could attract a super opportunity or you might get involved in a venture that will work out really well. If you don't have anything to look forward to over the next few months, start making some exciting plans. The thought of travel will never be far from your mind now, so how about booking up a holiday?

• *Friday 24 January* •

You're eager to learn more about the world today, especially if you discover something interesting or unusual. You could be attracted to a philosophy or religion that is slightly out of the ordinary, or want to know more about a campaign to make the world a better place. Other people may think your views are unconventional but they are unlikely to be so threatened by them that they get annoyed with you.

• *Saturday 25 January* •

Watch out today because someone in authority will try to lay down the law. They might issue an order and expect you to jump to it, or they may simply be very bossy and imply that they know best. This will get up your nose in no time at all, making you rather argumentative. You will also be determined to thwart them and not do what they say. This could be tricky if it's your boss that you're defying!

• *Sunday 26 January* •

Blow away the cobwebs today by getting engrossed in a leisure pursuit or hobby. You'll enjoy channelling all your energies into it so you don't have time to think about anything else. If you're participating in a group activity, you may have to take the lead in some way, whether or not you were expecting to do so. You will also be inspired to push ahead with a plan for the future.

• *Monday 27 January* •

You're keen to get on well with everyone around you today, even if you don't particularly like them. You don't want to seem petty or small-minded, so you'll do your best to give people the benefit of the doubt if necessary. If you've been considering joining a club or society but haven't been sure whether it's a good idea, you might decide to take the plunge now.

• *Tuesday 28 January* •

Being with other people will do you the world of good today. They'll cheer you up if you need it and they may also remind you to count your blessings if you've forgotten about them recently. You'll certainly have a good laugh together. You could hear from a chum who lives overseas, especially if they're planning to visit you.

• *Wednesday 29 January* •

There's a distinct gulf between you and a certain person today, and it soon gets you down. You might feel that they don't approve of you, perhaps because they're being critical or haughty. Try not to react by being equally distant or stuffy yourself, because that will only start a vicious circle. If things get really difficult you may have fantasies about severing all links with this person, but is that really an option?

• *Thursday 30 January* •

You're in a very compassionate and understanding mood today, enabling you to empathize with others and making you reluctant to judge them. You may even want to help people who are having a hard time. However, be careful because you aren't very discriminating at the moment and there is a small chance that someone might try to take you for a ride. So do your best to find a balance between being forgiving and being foolish.

• *Friday 31 January* •

This is a good day for immersing yourself in personal projects. You're very wrapped up in your own affairs now, giving you a chance to assess your progress and plan what your next step should be. However, you will expect everyone else to be equally interested in you, which could lead to disappointment if they have other things to think about.

FEBRUARY AT A GLANCE

Love	♥ ♥ ♥ ♥ ♥
Money	£ $ £ $ £
Career	💻 💻 💻 💻 💻
Health	☼ ☼ ☼ ☼ ☼

• *Saturday 1 February* •

February gets off to a great start, thanks to today's vibrant New Moon. This not only heralds the start of the Chinese New Year of the Goat but also indicates the beginning of an exciting fortnight for you. You will feel energetic and enthusiastic, which is just what you need if you want to kick-start a project or take a new direction in your life. It's also a terrific chance to start a diet or find some other way of improving your image or appearance.

• *Sunday 2 February* •

A certain person is very full of themselves today. They're radiating enthusiasm and optimism, but you may decide that a little goes a long way. On the other hand, maybe someone thinks this about you? If so, try to put the brakes on a bit and not come on too strong. If you've been having problems with a partner recently, this is a brilliant chance to jolly them out of their current mood and put matters to rights.

• *Monday 3 February* •

A friend is very fired up today, and as a result they'll quickly get impatient or argumentative. This is especially likely if money or possessions enter the equation. If you're currently trying to arrange a forthcoming social event, there could be a difference of opinion about how much it should cost or where it will be held. Should you stand your ground or cave in to the opposition?

• *Tuesday 4 February* •

There's a delicious scent of romance in the air between now and this time next month, and you could be swept off your feet by a certain person. You may already know exactly who this is or it could come as a wonderful surprise. This will also be a terrific chance to enjoy some time to yourself, so perhaps you can pamper yourself to the hilt or get on with a favourite activity undisturbed.

• *Wednesday 5 February* •

It's a super day for getting on well with other people, especially if you're all working together as part of a team. If you want to persuade someone to see things from your point of view, this is the day to do it: your enthusiasm will soon rub off on everyone you talk to yet you won't be too overpowering. It's also a good opportunity to take a leading role in a group activity.

• *Thursday 6 February* •

You're in a very sociable mood today and will really enjoy talking to whoever happens to be around. It's a great day for getting on well with neighbours, close relatives and anyone else who you see on a regular basis. This is also a good opportunity to assess the progress you're making in personal projects, and to make sure that you're on the right track.

• *Friday 7 February* •

Someone has some advice for you today, so listen carefully. They may be able to point you in the right direction over something or give you words of wisdom. Alternatively, you might read something interesting or useful, perhaps in a newspaper or book. If you're planning a social event or party, you'll enjoy getting down to the nitty-gritty of it all now.

• Saturday 8 February •

Get to grips with a future hope or dream today by analysing it in a lot of detail. How feasible is it and do you still want it to happen? Don't be shy about making changes or adjustments now, even if they mean that you have to start again from scratch or revise all your plans. If you've been having problems with a friend lately, this is a good chance to talk through your differences and find some common ground.

• Sunday 9 February •

Someone is being awfully defensive today, and they could take everything you say the wrong way because they're apparently so keen to feel aggrieved or offended. This is especially likely if you commit the cardinal sin of being rude about their past or their family, or of disparaging their home in some way. If you've been considering buying some property you may change your mind about it now.

• Monday 10 February •

The more predictable the day threatens to be, the more eager you will be to liven things up in some way. Try to do this before you start getting fed up or bored, because once that happens you'll have a tendency to stir up trouble just to see what happens next. Perhaps this is a good time to make some imaginative changes to your home or domestic set-up, so it will be more interesting in future?

• Tuesday 11 February •

A loved one is a tremendous support today, and it's good to know that you can rely on them so heavily. They might prop you up when you need it or let you know that they're behind you one hundred per cent. This is a fantastic day for getting on with a creative or artistic project because you'll be inspired without losing sight of your main aim. As a result, you'll make a lot of progress.

• *Wednesday 12 February* •

Get together with some of your favourite people today, even if you can't spare much time for them. It will do your heart good to see them. If you fancy going out on the town, you'll enjoy going to the cinema or theatre. If you've recently fallen for someone and you're wondering if it's reciprocal, you could get the answer you've been hoping for now.

• *Thursday 13 February* •

You're in a very talkative frame of mind until early March, and will really enjoy chatting about anything in which you have a personal interest. Unfortunately you won't be so keen on talking about things that have little to do with you, even if they fascinate everyone else. It will also be a good opportunity to put your thoughts into words, whether on paper or in the course of conversation.

• *Friday 14 February* •

Try to hold off from starting any new projects at work today because they could turn out to be a waste of time, or you may have to scrap what you've done and start again another day. Instead, try to continue what you have already begun. If you've been toying with the idea of going on a diet, don't start it today – you'll soon get fed up with it.

• *Saturday 15 February* •

If you're talking to someone today, don't be surprised if they get bogged down in lots of detail and lose track of what they were saying. They may even get totally sidelined by petty considerations and the sort of nit-picking that drives you mad. You might also lose your patience with a partner, so you end up squabbling with each other about all sorts of silly things. Try to keep calm!

• Sunday 16 February •

The higher the pedestal you've put someone on, the more likely they are to fall off it today. It's a difficult day when your faith in someone is put to the test, but the question will be whether this is because they've let you down in some way or you've expected too much from them. Do your best to remain objective and to avoid getting drawn into making moral judgements.

• Monday 17 February •

You're at great pains to show a different side of yourself today. In fact, the more someone wants to put you into a neat pigeon-hole, the more you'll want to break free and show that you aren't like this at all. If things get tough, you'll also want to prove your independence in some way but try not to hurt anyone's feelings in the process. Surely you can spread your wings without breaking hearts?

• Tuesday 18 February •

If you've been trying to keep quiet about something, it could all come out in the wash today. For instance, if you've been hoping that your partner wouldn't notice how much money you've taken out of the joint account, they could hit the roof now when they finally get round to looking at your bank statements. There could also be red faces over someone's sex life.

• *Wednesday 19 February* •

Money, possessions and material security will carry a lot of significance for you during the next four weeks, and you may even place much more importance on them than usual. It will be tempting to judge people by what they own rather than who they are, making you wary of anyone who doesn't have many status symbols. You may have to remind yourself that there's more to life than cash.

• *Thursday 20 February* •

Someone has some big ideas today and they aren't afraid to talk about them. As you listen, you may want to pinch yourself because you can't believe what you're hearing. You might think it's overblown nonsense, pie in the sky or a string of fanciful exaggerations. Or do you lack the vision to appreciate this person's ideas? Maybe you should hedge your bets for the time being.

• *Friday 21 February* •

This is a fantastic day for using your imagination because you'll be totally inspired. But it won't be nearly so good for keeping track of complicated ideas or doing anything very detailed, because your mind will drift all over the place and you'll get confused. You might also be rather absent-minded when it comes to doing mundane things, so be wary of leaving things behind or forgetting something important.

• *Saturday 22 February* •

Mind how you go when dealing with older friends and relatives today. Someone might become rather haughty or too full of themselves, so it's almost impossible to have a sensible conversation with them. Unfortunately, it will be awfully tempting to get your emotions and your thoughts mixed up, so you become too subjective. If this happens it will be a struggle to retain your customary rational outlook.

• Sunday 23 February •

Mix business and pleasure at your peril today because the result could be a lot of bad feeling. It isn't much better when combining friends and finances, such as in a social activity, because some people may object to the amount of expense involved. If you're currently feeling the pinch, you won't be very pleased or impressed if a certain person starts showing off or bragging about their possessions. Grrr!

• Monday 24 February •

This is a lovely day for being with people on the same wavelength as you. It will do you good to be with them and to have conversations in which you agree wholeheartedly about things. If you're currently involved in an altruistic or philanthropic venture, you'll want to do your bit to help now. You may also offer some assistance to a friend who's going through a bad time.

• Tuesday 25 February •

Someone's in a bit of a hurry today. They won't want to hang about and wait for anyone, and they'll also expect things to be done in double-quick time. Not surprisingly, this could soon lead to raised voices. For instance, if you're meeting a friend and turn up late, they might yell at you for keeping them waiting or may not even be there because they've stomped off in a huff. Whoops!

• Wednesday 26 February •

You've got a fantastic eye for detail today and will be very good at spotting what's going on. That might mean discerning the holes in someone's argument or realizing what your next step should be in a plan for the future. You're in an intellectual frame of mind now and will enjoy putting your brain to the test in any way that takes your fancy.

• *Thursday 27 February* •

You may not know it but you're being very seductive and sensual today. As a result, you're sending out some very sultry messages. Try to be aware of this so you don't attract any unwelcome attention. For instance, someone might give you a big come-on because they think you're giving them come-hither glances, when what you're really doing is staring into space or wondering about what to have for supper.

• *Friday 28 February* •

You're in quite a serious mood today and you certainly don't want to waste your time on anything that you consider to be frivolous or beneath your dignity. You may even prefer to keep quiet rather than get dragged into a silly gossip or some idle chat. However, it's a good chance to have a heart-to-heart with someone but beware of sounding too strict or formal.

MARCH AT A GLANCE

Love	♥ ♥			
Money	£ $ £ $ £			
Career	💻 💻 💻			
Health	☼ ☼ ☼			

• *Saturday 1 March* •

You've got a lot to talk about today so you're looking for an appreciative audience. However, they may not listen for very long if you can only talk about yourself and you show no interest in them. There needs to be some give and take! If you're on the phone to someone, you could run up a big bill by chatting for longer than you intended. If you're trying to economize, maybe you should send them an e-mail instead.

• *Sunday 2 March* •

You're in the mood to enhance or improve your image in some way during the next four weeks. So how are you going to do this? You might decide to have your hair styled differently, buy yourself some new make-up or have a blitz on the shops and buy some new clothes. You certainly like the idea of seeing a new you every time you look in the mirror, and you probably can't wait to get started.

• *Monday 3 March* •

Your finances are highlighted by today's New Moon, and they will remain so during the coming fortnight. This will be an excellent chance to make sure that all your money matters are up to date and that you haven't overlooked anything important. It will also be a good opportunity to consider making some sensible investments, whether these are modest or major. Big oaks can grow from tiny acorns . . .

• *Tuesday 4 March* •

You're in a very inventive frame of mind today and will enjoy thinking up all sorts of clever schemes. Try not to be downhearted if someone doesn't agree with you, because they may not be as forward-thinking as you. Don't discard any ideas, even if some of them don't seem feasible at the moment, because you never know when they might come in handy. Jot them down in case they whizz through your mind so fast that you forget them almost as quickly as they arrived.

• *Wednesday 5 March* •

The coming fortnight is an excellent chance to think seriously about your current financial situation. If you're having problems at the moment or you need some expert advice, now is the time to pick someone's brains and see what they've got to say. Alternatively, you might prefer to do your own research by reading financial magazines or the money pages in your newspaper.

• *Thursday 6 March* •

You're keen to have an in-depth conversation with someone today, especially if you need to get certain topics out into the open. You'll manage to be serious without becoming too sombre or dry. It's a nice day for tackling an artistic or creative task, and you'll want to do it to the very best of your ability. You'd rather take extra time over something than rush it and have to do it twice.

• *Friday 7 March* •

This is a delightful day for being with members of the family, especially if you're sharing a meal or doing something enjoyable together. Everyone will make a big effort to get on well with everyone else, although you should keep watch for a woman who may be feeling rather left out or who wants to remind everyone of how important she thinks she is.

• *Saturday 8 March* •

Thinking of going shopping today? You'll really enjoy looking for domestic items, whether that means scouring the shelves of your supermarket for edible goodies or buying a household appliance in a department store. You'll be drawn towards anything that will make you feel cosy or safe, and that goes for people too. If someone puts you at your ease, you'll want to be near them now.

• Sunday 9 March •

A certain person is being rather uppity today. They may take umbrage at all sorts of innocent remarks and events, or they might deliberately say something that puts the cat among the pigeons. Unfortunately, you won't be immune from this yourself, especially if you start to feel fed up or bored. The moment you begin to get crotchety, try to do something therapeutic – otherwise you'll want to cause havoc.

• Monday 10 March •

During the next few months there will be times when you'll question your priorities in life. You may wonder whether they are as important as you once thought, and you might even want to do something quite reckless out of sheer bravado. Don't block these thoughts because they could be very valuable, but equally you should try to avoid making any major decisions on the spur of the moment.

• Tuesday 11 March •

There could be a disagreement over money between you and a loved one today, so take care. You might object to what they spend their cash on, perhaps because you don't think it's suitable or it's a waste of money. There could also be resentment because one of you appears to be more fortunate than the other. Not only that, but someone's possessiveness may stick in your gullet now and lead to a row.

• Wednesday 12 March •

You're in a wonderfully idealistic mood today and you want only to dwell on topics that are pleasant. Anything else will soon be swept under the carpet, but make sure you return to it another time because it might be important. If you meet someone for the first time now you'll only see the good in them, and this will continue for the duration of your relation-ship.

• Thursday 13 March •

A certain someone is very strict and stern with you today, making you feel like a naughty child who's been made to stand in the corner. What have you done to deserve such harsh treatment? Actually, you may not have done much at all and this person could be over-reacting, or perhaps you're reading too much into the situation. But if you've overstepped the mark in some way, don't be too proud to apologize now.

• Friday 14 March •

Someone is surprisingly unhelpful today, especially if you're asking them to begin a new project. You won't get far with them at all, and you may decide that you might as well save your breath and try again another day. If you want to apply for a new job, try to resist the temptation to do so today because nothing may come of your application. But it could be a different story if you do it tomorrow.

• Saturday 15 March •

This is no day to go it alone because you'll get such a buzz from being with other people. You'll really enjoy any sort of social event, especially if it introduces you to some new people. You could really hit it off with someone you meet now, and you may even find that you share the same sense of humour so there is plenty to laugh about. It's also a super day for taking part in some form of team work.

• *Sunday 16 March* •

Someone or something arouses your curiosity today and you won't rest until you've got to the bottom of it. For instance, you might become suspicious about a friend's behaviour and be determined to find out what they're playing at. This could take up a lot of your time, especially if you don't immediately get the answers you're looking for. Try not to become irrational or lose your perspective about this.

• *Monday 17 March* •

Sort out your finances today, especially if you've overlooked something recently or have been avoiding tackling something unpleasant. You're in the mood to get on with it today, partly because you don't want to have to worry about it any longer. If you've spent too much money recently you could receive a nasty letter from your bank or a startling credit card bill, making you eager to start economizing.

• *Tuesday 18 March* •

Think about your official and joint finances during the coming two weeks, particularly if you want to make some sweeping changes to them. This will also be a good opportunity to pay attention to close and intimate relationships, and to check that things are running smoothly. If you've had problems over someone's jealousy or possessiveness lately, try to do something about it now.

• *Wednesday 19 March* •

A friend has a strong impact on you today, bringing the two of you closer together. It might even be the start of an important chapter in your relationship, perhaps uniting you on a very intense level. If you could do with some light relief after some of the things that have been happening to you recently, immerse yourself in a favourite hobby or spare-time pursuit.

• *Thursday 20 March* •

You're able to combine optimism with a sense of realism today, so you get the best of both worlds. It's a great day for getting on with any form of study or education, because your heart will be in it and you'll enjoy learning for its own sake. If you're about to take a test or exam, you'll have little reason to worry if you've done your homework and keep cool under fire.

• *Friday 21 March* •

The coming four weeks promise to be very lively and busy, and you'll feel as though you're at the centre of things. This will be invigorating and exciting, and you'll really enjoy being involved in whatever is going on around you. Do your best to get out and about as much as possible, because you'll enjoy having a change of scene every now and then. How about planning some day trips?

• *Saturday 22 March* •

If you want to widen your circle of friends, head for a local event or neighbourhood activity today. You could see some familiar faces but, more importantly, you might meet some potential new chums. If you don't have anything special planned for this weekend, you might suddenly be inspired to take off on a short trip. It will be fun to do something on the spur of the moment.

• *Sunday 23 March* •

You're in a thoughtful mood today although you won't be so wrapped up in your thoughts that you become antisocial.

Actually, you'll really enjoy talking to someone who's a kindred spirit, and you may well find that you think alike on some issues. Listen to your intuition now because it could give you some very interesting pointers or tell you how to deal with a certain person.

• *Monday 24 March* •

It's difficult to get close to a loved one today. That might be because they're nowhere to be seen or because they're being rather reserved and withdrawn. Try not to take this too seriously unless it's all part of a very familiar pattern that is making you increasingly unhappy. If it's a one-off, give this person the space they obviously need by doing things on your own for a while.

• *Tuesday 25 March* •

You're in a very outgoing and gregarious mood today, and you'll thoroughly enjoy being with other people. In fact, you'll feel like a fish out of water if you have to spend too long by yourself, and you'll probably end up spending hours on the phone or Internet instead. Listen to a friend or neighbour: they may have some brilliant ideas that spark off further inspiration in you.

• *Wednesday 26 March* •

If you're waiting for news about an allowance, grant or benefit to which you think you're entitled, chase it up now. However, this isn't a good day to make any new applications for such things because they won't get very far. They might become tangled up in a mass of red tape or they may even vanish altogether so you never hear another word about them.

• *Thursday 27 March* •

You'll have a tremendous appreciation for beauty during the coming four weeks and will enjoy being around things that delight the eye. You might decide to visit an art gallery at some point or you may want to spend a lot of time in a favourite piece of countryside. You'll also enjoy buying items that give you pleasure, even if they have no practical use.

• *Friday 28 March* •

If you get the chance to go shopping today you'll have a fine old time. You may also want to splash out on all sorts of impulse buys, whether you need them or not. If you're looking for some new clothes at the moment you might decide that you've seen the very thing, even if it isn't your usual style or it makes quite a statement. But will you still love it tomorrow? Better keep the receipt, just in case!

• *Saturday 29 March* •

You're in a very ebullient and positive mood today and it will soon rub off on everyone around you. This is a fabulous day to jazz up your social life by getting together with some lively friends. If you've been wondering whether to ask someone out, you might pluck up the courage now and be very glad that you did when they say yes.

• *Sunday 30 March* •

If possible, try to do something that you really enjoy today. You'll put a lot of energy into it and will feel good when you've finished it. Ideally, you should spend some time alone now because you'll enjoy your own company. This solitude may also give you the opportunity to think about some of your priorities in life and perhaps to decide to devote more time to them.

• *Monday 31 March* •

You belong to one of the most intellectual signs of all, as you enjoy proving today. You'll seize any excuse to put your brain through its paces, especially if that means looking deep into a subject and refusing to take it at face value. It's a good day for participating in a debate or discussion because you'll make some very interesting points and you'll enjoy being as rational and logical as possible.

APRIL AT A GLANCE

Love	♥ ♥ ♥
Money	£ $ £
Career	💻 💻
Health	☼ ☼ ☼ ☼

• *Tuesday 1 April* •

If you're been having problems with a certain someone recently, at least start to get them sorted out during the coming fortnight. Today's New Moon may enable you to talk this person round or make them see sense. It's also a marvellous opportunity to take part in a discussion or debate in which you have a vested interest. If you're thinking of doing some wheeling and dealing, get cracking now.

• *Wednesday 2 April* •

You're blessed with a big heart and an understanding nature today, which is super if you're trying to appreciate someone else's point of view. You're at great pains to meet people halfway rather than trying to impose your values and beliefs on them. A conversation with a close relative or someone else who you see on a regular basis will be very telling, and could bring you closer together.

• *Thursday 3 April* •

If you're going shopping today, don't be surprised if you bring back lots of items that weren't on your list. Yes, it's one of those days when you're in the mood to snap things up on impulse, even if you don't really need them. Well, you reason, you might need them one day and so it will be handy to have them standing by. If you enjoy experimenting with cooking, you might decide to buy some exotic or unusual ingredients now.

• *Friday 4 April* •

Someone is slightly too big for their boots today. This won't last long but it could get on your nerves in the meantime. You may also rack your brains trying to think up some way to burst this person's bubble or cut them down to size. If you're with the family or your other half, be prepared for them to tease you unmercifully if they think you're getting ideas above your station or are exaggerating about something.

• *Saturday 5 April* •

Between now and mid-June, there will be phases when your mind keeps straying back to the past. There may even be occasions when you're completely wrapped up in your memories and find it difficult to return to the present. This is a marvellous opportunity to look through your keepsakes and mementos, especially if you would really like to scale them down to a more manageable number.

• *Sunday 6 April* •

If you're currently stuck for inspiration about something, discuss it with members of the family today because they could come up with some brilliant ideas. Alternatively, it will work the other way round, with you coming up with a solution to someone's problems. If you're in the throes of moving house, you'll have some bright ideas about the logistics of what's involved.

• Monday 7 April •

Your social life is great fun today, so make the most of it whenever you get the chance. It's a terrific day for mixing with people who always make you feel good or who remind you that there's more to life than mundane chores and money worries. If you fancy giving yourself a treat, rent a video or take yourself off to the cinema. It will do you good!

• Tuesday 8 April •

You're in a domesticated mood today and will enjoy pottering about at home, making sure everything is in order. If you work from home, consider ways of making things more comfortable or organized now. Maybe you should rearrange the furniture slightly or make an alteration to your working hours? If you work with other people you'll enjoy having a chat with a colleague.

• Wednesday 9 April •

It's a tricky day because it's difficult to get things right. You could fall out with someone over some silly trifle or simply feel at odds with the world. You might also have to deal with people who are out of sorts or determined to have a row. Be very careful when talking to neighbours because it will be horribly easy to rub them up the wrong way, or vice versa. Not an easy day.

• Thursday 10 April •

A certain someone is full of ideas today, but are these any good or are they talking through their hat? Be wary if this person tries to talk you into things against your better judgement, or if they promise something that sounds too good to be true. They may be exaggerating, even if they aren't aware of it. However, they will be very persuasive so it could be difficult to resist them.

• Friday 11 April •

Do your best to be choosy about the company you keep today. Your ego isn't as strong as usual, so you could easily feel deflated by someone's unpleasant remarks or their tendency to put you down. If you're currently worried about the state of a relationship, things could really get to you now. But are you making mountains out of molehills? You may be reading too much into the situation.

• Saturday 12 April •

You're charm itself today, making it delightfully easy to get on well with whoever happens to be around. If someone needs buttering up, now is the time to do it provided you don't lay it on too thick. It's a super day for participating in local events and neighbourhood activities, because you'll enjoy feeling that you're at the centre of things. You might even make an interesting new contact.

• Sunday 13 April •

If you're currently having doubts about a domestic plan or family matter, things will really start to get to you today. Before you know it, you'll be picturing the worst unless you can keep a firm grip on your imagination. There could be an element of confusion between you and a loved one, perhaps when you disagree about something that happened in the past. Who's right and who's wrong?

• *Monday 14 April* •

You're very organized today so it's a great day for making things happen. If you're trying to arrange a forthcoming social event or celebration, this is a super opportunity to check that everything is going according to plan. You're great at issuing instructions now without appearing bossy. It's also a good day for having a heartfelt chat with a loved one.

• *Tuesday 15 April* •

The more open-minded you can be when talking to a certain someone today, the better your conversation will go. This is important if you're trying to get this person to see things from your point of view or are desperately trying to achieve some sort of compromise. Even when talking to people with very different opinions, you'll manage to respect their viewpoint while putting forward your own. Excellent!

• *Wednesday 16 April* •

The more entrenched a philosophy or belief is, the more doubts you'll have about it during the rest of April. Events that take place may make you question something that you've always taken for granted until now. This will be uncomfortable if you associate your ideas with your identity because you'll feel as though your whole existence is being called into question. However, it won't be so difficult if you can separate yourself from your beliefs because then you'll find it easier to scrutinize and reassess them.

• *Thursday 17 April* •

Watch out if you're mixing friends and finances today because things won't run very smoothly. You may suspect that a chum is trying to diddle you in some way, especially if they start using emotional blackmail to make you feel guilty or sorry for them. For instance, if the arrangement is that you'll buy something for them and they'll pay you back later, they may make an excuse about why they can't do this and then make you feel bad about expecting to get your money. Better not to get involved in the first place.

• *Friday 18 April* •

Oh boy! Someone's operating on a very short fuse today and if you're sensible you'll try to keep out of their way as much as possible. The slightest thing could set them off, especially if they discover something that you were hoping to keep under wraps. However, are you going to let them chew you out without standing up for yourself? This may lead to a row but you aren't prepared to be yelled at for no good reason.

• *Saturday 19 April* •

You and your money are soon parted today, especially if you're taking part in a group event or you're going shopping. You'll be tempted to splash out on all sorts of things, even if you don't really need them. Anyway, needing things isn't really the point because what you're really looking for is some excitement now. It may be cheaper to do something really wacky from the outset.

• *Sunday 20 April* •

You'll be very wrapped up in your home and family during the next four weeks, and you'll thoroughly enjoy being with loved ones whenever you get the chance. If your real family aren't around for some reason, get together with cherished friends instead. This will be a very good opportunity to reassess your current living conditions and to start thinking about any changes that you think are necessary.

• *Monday 21 April* •

You're powered by dynamic energy during the next two months, and it will be the perfect chance to push ahead with lots of projects and ideas. You don't want to stand around on the sidelines or hedge your bets any longer. Instead, you're anxious to take the plunge, even if things don't work out in quite the way you expect. You'll have a strong belief in yourself but it will still pay to listen to others as well.

• *Tuesday 22 April* •

Although you have a hankering for familiar faces and places at the moment, you aren't keen on anything that's too familiar today. In fact, you're in the mood for some excitement and will enjoy doing something for the first time. The events that take place now will challenge some of your ideas, making you reassess them from a fresh viewpoint. This will be very stimulating and exciting.

• *Wednesday 23 April* •

Tempers are easily frayed today, especially if someone accidentally treads on your toes or trespasses on your feelings. You're in rather a defensive mood, as you'll make more than plain when you get on your high horse. Do your best to keep control of your emotions or they will soon have control over you. If that happens, you'll quickly become emotionally exhausted and will get things out of proportion.

• *Thursday 24 April* •

After yesterday's outbursts, it's anything for a quiet life today. You're in a much more pacific mood and want to take things as easy as possible. If someone annoys you, you'll do your best to ignore it or put it down as one of those things. Your intuition is working strongly now so take note of your gut instincts, especially if they're telling you to take avoiding action about something.

• *Friday 25 April* •

No matter what else you're doing today, try to find the time for a creative or artistic activity. It will do you the world of good to forget about everything else and to immerse yourself in something that allows you full self-expression. This is also a lovely day for giving some moral support to a child or adolescent, or for giving them the benefit of your experience about something.

• *Saturday 26 April* •

You're in a home-loving mood today and will enjoy getting to grips with some domestic chores. You could even be inspired to work some culinary magic in the kitchen, perhaps making someone's favourite meal or baking yourself a gooey chocolate cake. Try to have a little time to yourself at some point so you can think about some of your priorities in life.

• *Sunday 27 April* •

It's a very sociable and outgoing day, especially if you can be with people who you know inside out. You'll enjoy nattering about whatever pops into your head, even if it's quite trivial. However, a loved one may have something specific that they want to talk about. You might enjoy recording the day for posterity, so get out your camera and take a few snaps for your photo album.

• *Monday 28 April* •

It's wonderfully easy to get on well with everyone around you today. If only every day were like this! You're full of grace, tact and humour, so don't be surprised if people cluster round you like wasps around a jam pot. If you need to do some spadework with someone to win them round, try to do it now while everything is working so well in your favour. How can they resist you?

• *Tuesday 29 April* •

You're capable of achieving a great deal today, especially if you push yourself harder than usual. The trick will be in knowing when to hit the brakes and when to move forward. You need to tread a fine line between being confident and cocky, and you also want to get people on your side rather than alienate them. Above all, avoid sounding self-righteous or arrogant, and then you'll be fine.

• *Wednesday 30 April* •

You long to liven things up a little today, so what do you have in mind? You certainly don't want to jog along as usual but you don't need to create havoc, either. Consider injecting some variety into your schedule or doing something on the spur of the moment. You might also hear some surprising but exciting news about a property deal or house move.

MAY AT A GLANCE

Love	♥ ♥ ♥ ♥ ♥
Money	£ $
Career	💻 💻
Health	☼ ☼ ☼

• *Thursday 1 May* •

The month gets off to an invigorating start, thanks to today's New Moon. You'll feel the effects of this during the coming fortnight, especially if you concentrate on your domestic life.

It's a great chance to begin afresh with someone dear to your heart if things have been a bit dicey between you lately. If you're in the throes of moving house and are wondering when you'll get a completion date, things could soon start to happen fast.

• *Friday 2 May* •

You're in a very understanding and gentle mood today, making you a nice person to have around. If there's been a rift with someone recently or you've been having lots of petty squabbles, you'll be at pains now to restore the peace and put the whole thing behind you. It will do you good to be in some beautiful and harmonious surroundings at some point, especially if they are near water.

• *Saturday 3 May* •

It's an energy-packed day and you'll enjoy making the most of it. You won't want to take things easy unless you have little choice in the matter because you're in such a dynamic mood. Ideally, you should get together with some of your favourite people and do something exciting. You'll also enjoy being physically active, whether you have a session at the gym, jog round the block or dance the night away.

• *Sunday 4 May* •

You could hear some disappointing news today, especially if it concerns a loved one or a property. Try not to let this affect you more than necessary, because it's one of those days when your spirits will start to sink with little provocation. Be careful when dealing with a member of the family who seems determined to puncture your ego or play the martyr.

• *Monday 5 May* •

You're in a very constructive and practical mood today, and you don't want to be deterred from the task in hand. It's a great day for rolling up your sleeves and getting on with whatever needs to be done, especially if it involves organizing other people in some way. Your creative powers are looking pretty good, too, so it's a great day for turning your hand to something artistic.

• *Tuesday 6 May* •

It's another day when you're in the mood to make things happen, but today you want to concentrate on domestic and work tasks. If you're at home you might decide to have a blitz on the cleaning or to do some tidying up. If you're at work, you'll enjoy doing some filing or anything else that will ensure you're at your most efficient. But try to have a break at some point. Otherwise you'll wear yourself out.

• *Wednesday 7 May* •

This is a super day for getting in touch with members of the family, whether that means dropping in on someone for a cup of tea or ringing up a relative who lives a long way away. You'll really enjoy talking about the past, especially if you're chatting to someone who shared the experiences with you. However, this person may hog the conversation if you give them half a chance.

• *Thursday 8 May* •

Someone is being rather headstrong and domineering today, and you may decide that you'd like to limit the amount of time you spend with them to avoid being browbeaten. They may try to talk you into doing something that they want, in which case they won't shut up until they've got their own way. They may also persuade you to join them in an activity that you think sounds too risky for words. Be careful!

• *Friday 9 May* •

There's a lot of friction between you and a certain someone today, and it won't be easy to cope with. You may keep rubbing each other up the wrong way so you have lots of arguments, or one of you might go into a massive sulk so there's a nasty silence. If one of you is simmering with fury over a past grievance, try to get things out into the open. You don't want to continue this feud any longer than necessary.

• *Saturday 10 May* •

Be very careful when handling money today because you'll be tempted to splash out on all sorts of items that you don't really need. You might also go mad with the joint account, or maybe your other half will do that. If you're getting bored with your sex life, this is a good day to liven things up but be careful how you do it. Don't dent your partner's ego by saying hurtful things to them, just to get a rise out of them.

• *Sunday 11 May* •

Surround yourself with loved ones whenever you get the chance today. You'll enjoy making a fuss of them and you hope they'll return the favour. If you're in the middle of a house move, or it's something that you're considering, this is a good day to talk things over with the other people involved or to pick the brains of someone whose opinion you respect.

• *Monday 12 May* •

Someone has a rather unreliable memory today, as you will soon discover. They may remind you of things that ring absolutely no bells with you even though you were supposed to have been there at the time. Or they might develop a ridiculously rosy view of the past so they become nostalgic about something that never really happened. Make sure you don't fall into a similar trap yourself!

• Tuesday 13 May •

A certain person is a bit quick off the mark today when it comes to losing their temper. You may even get the impression that you can't even open your mouth without this person jumping down your throat. But is that really true? Although you may not be aware of it, you may be unconsciously winding this person up through your words or actions. Be especially careful of deliberately goading them into losing their temper.

• Wednesday 14 May •

It's a strange day. You're eager to get on with things yet you can't work up the energy. As a result, you'll soon start to feel irritable and edgy, yet you won't know why. Try to avoid making plans or taking action over anything important because your judgement isn't very accurate at the moment and you may end up doing things that you'll regret later on. Do something physical or therapeutic instead.

• Thursday 15 May •

You-know-who really loves the sound of their own voice, don't they? They'll ramble on today as though you've got nothing better to do than listen to them. They may also seize the chance to do a bit of showing off, perhaps by dropping names or bragging about their past triumphs. You'll probably tolerate them with good humour because you'll realize that they don't mean any harm by it. It may even be quite amusing.

• *Friday 16 May* •

Be prepared to make some important decisions during the rest of the month, especially where your home and career are concerned. That's because of today's eclipsed Full Moon, which will increase the emotional temperature. At times, you could feel quite het up or tearful, especially if matters seem out of your hands. Do your best not to let these feelings get out of control.

• *Saturday 17 May* •

A friend has a powerful impact on you today. They may say or do something that affects you deeply or which really makes you think. If you've been wondering whether you're falling in love with them, what happens between you now may offer conclusive proof that something is definitely going on. However, try not to get carried away now unless you're sure of your ground and of them.

• *Sunday 18 May* •

You fancy doing things on the spur of the moment today, especially if you're in need of a little excitement. If your Sundays always follow a predictable pattern, try to ring the changes in some way now, even if they're really quite modest. You don't feel the need to turn your world upside down but you could definitely do with spicing it up a little. Mind you, a member of the family may do this for you any moment now . . .

• *Monday 19 May* •

If you're trying to make plans for your home at the moment, someone could get rather carried away and make some very grandiose suggestions today. Well, they seem grandiose to you but there's a chance that they might be just what the doctor ordered. The question will be whether you're prepared to give them a go or you'd prefer to play safe. It's up to you . . .

• Tuesday 20 May •

This is a super day for enjoying your home comforts whenever you get the chance. You'll love the idea of lazing around at home or in the garden, preferably with some of your nearest and dearest not too far away. You're exuding a very peaceful energy at the moment, so don't be surprised if someone starts to confide in you about something that's been on their mind. You'll be happy to listen.

• Wednesday 21 May •

Life will have a lot to offer during the coming four weeks, especially where love, laughter and leisure are concerned. This is your chance to kick up your heels and have as much fun as possible. You'll be blessed with oodles of self-confidence, which will help to get you noticed. If you've been wondering when Mr or Ms Right will come along, keep your eyes peeled – you could spot them soon.

• Thursday 22 May •

Try to spend time with one of your favourite people today because you'll get a big kick out of them. They'll help to take you out of yourself and they may also give you some encouragement. You'll know this isn't idle flattery because they aren't that sort of person, so you'll be quite justified in feeling proud of yourself. You could also hear some words of wisdom from a child or teenager. How touching!

• *Friday 23 May* •

The more you love someone, the more likely you are to have problems with them today. They may get on your nerves or try to boss you about, or it might just be one of those aggravating days when you wind each other up like coiled springs. There could also be a lot of hassle if one of you is feeling possessive or insecure, because you'll want to cling to the other one like a piece of chewing gum. This won't go down well.

• *Saturday 24 May* •

You have a strong craving for excitement today and you won't be satisfied until something remarkable happens. Try to do things on impulse if you get the chance, or abandon your usual routine for something entirely new. If you doggedly persist with your normal Saturday schedule without any room for manoeuvre, you'll soon want to tear your hair out with frustration.

• *Sunday 25 May* •

A friend has some very strong ideas today and they won't want to be deflected from them. They'll try to talk you into seeing things from their point of view and you'll feel that you don't have much choice in the matter. If something has been brewing between you and a chum, the emotional temperature will rise by another couple of degrees today, making you wonder what your next step should be.

• *Monday 26 May* •

You're in a wonderfully gregarious and open-hearted mood today. You'll want to mix with as many people as possible, and also to shower them with affection. But be careful if you're with someone who you aren't very keen on because you could give them the impression that you're their number one fan. You don't want them coming on strong and making a nuisance of themselves.

• *Tuesday 27 May* •

If you're busy dreaming up new decorative schemes for your home or a new design for your garden, you'll be keen to get on with things today. You're in the mood to be inspired, so leaf through some magazines or books to spark off some ideas. Don't be shy about expressing your artistic abilities now! This is also a lovely day for having an in-depth conversation with one of the family or a close friend.

• *Wednesday 28 May* •

Someone dear to your heart is a bit muddled today. They may get the wrong end of the stick, mishear something or be living in a world of their own. However, until you realize this you might have the sort of frustrating conversation in which you go round in circles. You're also slightly distracted now, especially if you're preoccupied with worries about someone or something. Try to keep calm.

• *Thursday 29 May* •

You'll want to batten down the hatches today when a certain someone gets agitated. They could do a lot of shouting or just generally stamp around and make everyone quake in their boots. Unfortunately you could soon become infected by the same problem, making you irritable and snappy. Try not to take out your ire on people who don't deserve it.

• *Friday 30 May* •

Watch out if you're going shopping today because you're in the mood to spend money. That's fine if you've got lots to spare but it isn't such good news if you're currently trying to economize. Perhaps you're really interested in having some excitement and are doing this through a little retail therapy? If so, it may help to limit yourself to a certain amount of money and not allow yourself to exceed it.

• Saturday 31 May •

Today's eclipsed New Moon will have an invigorating effect on your love life during the next few weeks. You could fall head over heels with a certain person, whether that means falling in love again with your current partner or being totally smitten by someone new. There could be some exciting news about a child, and you may also be invited to a wonderful celebration or party. There's so much to look forward to!

JUNE AT A GLANCE

Love	♥	♥	♥	♥	♥
Money	£	$	£		
Career	💻	💻	💻	💻	💻
Health	☼	☼	☼	☼	☼

• Sunday 1 June •

You start the month in great form. You're eager to get things moving and are on the hunt for excitement. If you fancy someone at the moment and have been wondering when to make your move, you could get a lot of encouragement from this person now. It may even spur you into asking them out or making a big play for them. If you're already spoken for, you'll be in a very seductive mood with your other half.

• *Monday 2 June* •

You could hear some surprise news about your job or finances today. Alternatively, the two could be combined in some way. For instance, you might discover that you're in line for a pay rise or someone could be so pleased with your efforts that they give you a bonus or big tip. You might also have interesting developments with a colleague.

• *Tuesday 3 June* •

Back in February, your faith in someone was called into question and today you have further reason for doubting them. Maybe they've reneged on a promise that they made to you and you're bitterly disappointed, or perhaps you were expecting too much from them in the first place. It will be difficult to know whether you've raised your hopes too high or whether this person has let you down flat. Either way, it won't be a very easy experience but you'll make it even more stressful if you build it up into a massive crisis.

• *Wednesday 4 June* •

From today, you enter a new phase in your working life. Over the next couple of years you'll be kept very busy in your job, and there may even be times when you have to work extra hard to keep abreast of everything that's expected of you. If you've got your eye on a particular goal you'll stand a good chance of achieving it, but don't make it at the expense of your health. Slow down every now and then!

• *Thursday 5 June* •

There's a lot of tension between you and a loved one today, leading to a rather tricky atmosphere at times. You could have a blazing row but at least it will be a chance to clear the air and get things out into the open. Do your best not to allow recriminations or resentments to fester inside you because that will cause more problems in the long run. Instead, have things out with the relevant person now.

• Friday 6 June •

Go carefully because it's one of those tricky days when you can't settle to anything for long. If someone tries to tell you what to do, or they're being very possessive, you'll want to rebel in as dramatic a way as possible in order to get your message across. This will only be a fleeting mood but it won't be much fun while it lasts. Try not to make it worse than necessary.

• Saturday 7 June •

Someone thinks they know best but you beg to differ. This will soon result in a stalemate, with neither of you willing to back down, unless you can make the monumental effort to see things from their point of view or to agree to compromise. Emotional tension is building up inside you now, so try to release it by doing something physical or therapeutic. Otherwise you'll go off pop!

• Sunday 8 June •

A certain person is a stickler for accuracy and precision today. They'll quickly point out your mistakes and will make you feel like a naughty child who's got to stand in the corner wearing a dunce's cap. Are they being reasonable? Or are they imposing such high standards on you that only a saint could meet them? You may feel aggrieved but try not to act as though you're a martyr.

• *Monday 9 June* •

Take care when handling friends today because someone could get above themselves. They may do their best to boss you about or they might try to impose their will on you. You won't like this one bit and will feel justified in saying so. However, make sure you don't unwittingly behave in the same manner by being too domineering or controlling of other people. Try to live and let live.

• *Tuesday 10 June* •

Between now and early July you'll want to have as much enjoyment as possible. And it looks as though you'll get your wish because you'll be very popular and in great demand socially. If you've been hoping to win someone's heart, your wish could soon be granted when it becomes obvious that they're putty in your hands. You'll also have a wonderful time expressing some of your creative talents now.

• *Wednesday 11 June* •

You'd better grow another layer of skin quickly or wrap yourself in cotton wool today, otherwise a certain someone could say something very hurtful or unfair. Unfortunately, they seem to be shooting from the hip and don't care if their words have a powerful impact on your feelings. Before you give them a taste of their own medicine, try to find out what's wrong. It may put a different complexion on things.

• *Thursday 12 June* •

A loved one has a few surprises up their sleeve today, as you'll soon discover. They may drop a bombshell that leaves you reeling, or make it obvious that they need to be given their head for a while. If you've never found a certain person attractive in the past, you might be staggered to discover that they're suddenly making you weak at the knees. Where do you go from here?

• *Friday 13 June* •

Between now and the end of the month you'll get a lot of fun from using your brain. Let's face it, you're no intellectual slouch at the best of times so you'll be really clever throughout the rest of June. You might also be feeling lucky, so how about entering some competitions or taking part in a quiz? Don't tell yourself that you never win because there's always a first time for everything.

• *Saturday 14 June* •

Your relationship with a friend could undergo some important changes during the coming fortnight. If you've been annoyed with them recently you might now work things out between you or you may decide that you don't want to have anything more to do with them. This will also be a good opportunity to think about your hopes and plans for the future, and to decide whether they're still viable.

• *Sunday 15 June* •

Take things gently today otherwise you'll wear yourself out in no time at all. That's because you don't have as much stamina or energy as usual. The situation isn't helped by the fact that you're feeling ultra-responsible and won't want to let anyone down, so you may push yourself further than usual. But what good will you be to anyone if you're flat on your back or completely worn out?

• Monday 16 June •

Do your best to find some private time today in which you can be left to your own devices. It will do you the world of good to catch your breath and have a rest. You might even be inspired to do some meditation or creative visualization in an effort to make yourself feel better. If you're currently involved in a charity or good cause, don't start any new projects today: they won't get very far.

• Tuesday 17 June •

You may not consider yourself to be very materialistic but you could surprise yourself at times during the next few months. You may have phases when you are consumed with the idea of making money or when you will fight for what you think is yours. If you've been considering buying a new car or motor-bike, it will be almost impossible to resist temptation now.

• Wednesday 18 June •

You're in a very gregarious and sociable mood today, and you'll love being with other people whenever you get the chance. Not only are they good company in their own right, they'll help you to forget any hassles that you are currently facing. However, you won't take kindly to anyone who tries to restrict your movements or impinge on your personal freedom, as you'll make more than obvious.

• Thursday 19 June •

The atmosphere between you and your beloved is almost too good to be true today. You can't get enough of each other's company and you'll manage to rise above any petty irritations that normally get you down. It's the perfect opportunity to get dolled up and go out on the town together. Or maybe you'd rather stay in? You're also in the mood for drama and will adore the chance to show off at some point.

• *Friday 20 June* •

Once again you're basking in a wave of contentment and happiness, especially when you look at a certain person. If you meet someone for the first time now you could be totally smitten by them, and will only see their good points. This is fine if their good points outweigh their bad, but could cause trouble if you delude yourself that this person is something they're not.

• *Saturday 21 June* •

The next four weeks will find you in an industrious and businesslike mood, particularly when it comes to your job and being of service to people. You won't want to let yourself down by giving a bad impression or not doing things properly, although there is little chance of that at the moment. If you're considering looking for a new job, things will work in your favour now.

• *Sunday 22 June* •

You'll have a super time bouncing your ideas off other people today, and the results could be quite inspiring. For instance, you may encourage each other into having some fantastic brainwaves that might never have occurred to you otherwise. This is also a great day for making contact with people who you haven't seen for a while, or for catching up with your e-mail correspondence.

• *Monday 23 June* •

You're eager to do things on the spur of the moment today, particularly when it comes to parting with your cash. Actually, you're feeling pretty reckless and could easily decide to cast caution to the winds, along with your credit card or cheque-book. If someone is determined to stop you or keeps nagging you about being more prudent, you'll want to teach them a lesson by going totally over the top. Whoops!

• Tuesday 24 June •

You manage to combine practicality with brilliance today, and everyone else will only be able to stand back in amazement. It's an especially good day if you want to make a big impression on someone at work because you'll have no problems with this at all. If you're going near the shops you might be interested in items that will boost your health or improve your well-being in some way.

• Wednesday 25 June •

A so-called loved one really knows how to put the squeeze on you today. They could leave you at the mercy of their emotional demands, especially if they're being unreasonable. For instance, they may try to blackmail you into conceding to their wishes. Or will it be the other way round? Perhaps you're doing your best to impose your will on someone else, and are absolutely determined to get your own way?

• Thursday 26 June •

You won't like it if a loved one acts as though you're their personal possession today. In fact, you'll put your foot down very firmly and will be very vociferous on the subject. Take care when handling children and adolescents because they're very strong-willed now and won't take kindly to any efforts on your part to control them or make them behave themselves if they don't want to.

• *Friday 27 June* •

After yesterday's outbursts, it will be a relief to have a much more peaceful time today. You're keen to keep people sweet now, and will bend over backwards to pacify them if necessary. You are also perfectly able to rise above your differences with others because you're so keen to be magnanimous and big-hearted. This won't go unnoticed by a certain someone.

• *Saturday 28 June* •

Love makes your world go round today, and you won't be able to get enough of you-know-who. If you've been admiring someone from afar, this is your cue to make a big play for them. It's also a super day for doing something that brings out your creative talents, whether you're appreciating someone else's artistic prowess or are busy demonstrating your own.

• *Sunday 29 June* •

Are some changes needed to your job or working conditions? If so, start to set things in motion during the coming fortnight when things will go your way. This will also be an excellent time to consider ways of improving your health. If your job has been undermining your health, perhaps because you're rushed off your feet, think about how you can remedy the situation even if you start off very modestly.

• *Monday 30 June* •

You're very inventive and clever today, and you'll enjoy giving your brain a good workout. If you're currently tussling with a difficult or intransigent problem, you could suddenly hit on a solution now, especially if you use a bit of lateral thinking. Try the same sort of tactic if you're fed up with an ailment that doesn't want to go away. Perhaps it's time to try a complementary therapy if conventional medicine hasn't been able to help the problem.

JULY AT A GLANCE

Love	♥ ♥ ♥ ♥ ♥
Money	£ $ £
Career	💻 💻 💻 💻 💻
Health	☼ ☼ ☼ ☼ ☼

• Tuesday 1 July •

It's a powerful start to the month because you're feeling in control of things. In fact, you feel on top of everything and capable of achieving a tremendous amount now. This is a perfect opportunity to dust off some of your hopes and wishes for the future, and to get cracking on them. Don't keep putting them off – get started on something now and give it all your energy and focus.

• Wednesday 2 July •

You're in a forceful and dynamic mood today, and you'll really enjoy getting things moving. If you've been meaning to get round to arranging an appointment with your doctor or dentist, make sure you do it now while the thought is uppermost in your mind. This is also a good day for sorting out a budget or list of expenses connected with your work.

• Thursday 3 July •

This is a super day for being with other people because you're feeling so convivial and you'll be delighted to discover how popular you are. This is just what you need if you've been intending to fix up some social arrangements, such as getting together with a friend. It's also a lovely day for being with some of your favourite people. Or perhaps you're only interested in one of them at the moment?

• Friday 4 July •

During the rest of the month you'll take pleasure in doing your best at work. You'll want to help people whenever possible, whether it's expected of you or not. There could also be some delicious romance to make you more eager to go into work every day. For instance, you might take a shine to a colleague or start a flirtation with a customer. Even if it's harmless fun it will do wonders for your ego.

• Saturday 5 July •

Someone is in a very talkative mood today, so be warned! Once they get chatting it may be very difficult to tear yourself away, simply because you can't get a word in edgeways to say goodbye. They may regale you with lots of tales about their health, which will be another reason why it's difficult to make your excuses and leave. If you're at work, you'll have a chatty colleague or customer.

• Sunday 6 July •

You're in the mood to do things a little bit differently from usual today. You don't want to be completely radical but you'll enjoy the chance to ring the changes in some way. If you're currently thinking about investing in ways to improve your health, you'll be attracted by something that sounds unusual or unconventional, or which you've never tried before. Maybe it's time for an experiment?

• *Monday 7 July* •

It's one of those difficult days when it's hard to keep your patience for long. People seem to keep rubbing you up the wrong way, or perhaps it's six of one and half a dozen of the other? For instance, you may think that you're the injured party when actually you're being equally irritating in your own way. Try to avoid talking about politics or religion because these could turn out to be flashpoints.

• *Tuesday 8 July* •

Work commitments could come between you and a special person today. They may be too busy with other things to spare much time for you, or perhaps you're the one who has prior commitments and whose social life has to go by the wayside. You're also prone to anxiety now, but try not to let things get on top of you, because once that happens you'll find it hard to switch off.

• *Wednesday 9 July* •

This is a fantastic day for making a lot of progress at work, because you're in such an industrious and efficient frame of mind. What's more, you want to do things properly and aren't interested in cutting corners. It's a terrific opportunity to display your talents to people in authority, especially if you hope they might improve your career opportunities in some way. How can anyone fail to be impressed by you right now?

• *Thursday 10 July* •

You're in a restless mood today and can't bear the thought of anything or anyone that seems mundane or boring. Instead, you're looking for excitement and want to liven things up as much as possible. If you're feeling fed up, your instincts will tell you to spend some money, especially if you splash out on things that are unusual.

• *Friday 11 July* •

Sparks are flying between you and a certain person today, but for all the right reasons. There seems to be a strong attraction flowing between you, making it exciting to be around one another. You may not want to do anything about this but it will be good fun. This is also a super day for getting on with any jobs that are on your list of things to do because you've got so much energy and vitality now.

• *Saturday 12 July* •

Your spirits take a bit of a nosedive today, so look after yourself. You may feel as though you're dragging yourself around, because you have little or no energy. You might also feel as though you've got the weight of the world on your shoulders, and that everything is getting to you. The likelihood is that you're taking everything much more seriously than necessary, so try to find some light relief.

• *Sunday 13 July* •

During the next few weeks, it will be surprisingly easy to get your point across when talking to partners. This is because your powers of communication will be increased, and also because you will be at pains to listen to what others have to say. This will be a winning combination, and just what you need whenever you take part in a discussion or meeting. You'll want everyone to get a fair hearing now.

• *Monday 14 July* •

Be careful when talking to a certain person today because they could easily let their mind run away with them. As a result, they'll get het up about all sorts of silly things, and they may also lose sight of what is important. If you're having a conversation with someone, try to stick to the main points. Otherwise you could become sidetracked by time-wasting details.

• *Tuesday 15 July* •

Someone is full of confidence today and their positive attitude will soon rub off on you. However, try not to let them talk you into anything that is foolish or falsely optimistic, because you'll kick yourself later on. They may also exaggerate about the benefits of something that they want you to participate in but which may not be quite as beneficial as they are making out.

• *Wednesday 16 July* •

You're in rather a reckless mood today, especially when it comes to handling your finances. You might decide to splash out on something even though you can't afford it or you aren't sure if you've got enough money in the bank to cover it. You may also want to buy something because of the effect it will have on everyone else, especially if it promises to cause raised eyebrows.

• *Thursday 17 July* •

There's a good rapport between you and a certain person today, especially if you can help each other out in some way. For example, one of you might do the other one a favour or pay them a compliment. If you're working with someone as part of a team, you'll want to do your very best now to create a harmonious relationship between you.

• *Friday 18 July* •

It's another day when you're working well with other people and you'll take real pride in what you're doing. You'll excel at anything that displays your organizational skills or enables you to remind everyone what an asset you are. If you're currently on the hunt for a new job, you could find something that seems right up your street now.

• *Saturday 19 July* •

Someone could get their wires crossed today, leaving you in the dark or mystified about what's going on with them. They might be sending you some very mixed messages, so you aren't sure where you stand, or they may change their mind about something so frequently that you're almost dizzy. However, you may not be immune from this sort of thing yourself, especially if you're trying to hedge your bets or sit on the fence about something. You could leave someone wreathed in confusion if you aren't careful.

• *Sunday 20 July* •

You're in a very jaunty and gregarious mood today, and you'll welcome the chance to be as sociable as possible. You'll also manage to cheer people up with your presence, or maybe it's your jokes that get them laughing. If you want to jolly someone out of their bad mood or use your charm to stop them feeling angry with you, it shouldn't be difficult at all now. You'll manage it effortlessly.

• *Monday 21 July* •

Someone is operating on a very short fuse today, especially if they're busy with lots of chores or they're up to their ears in work. Perhaps that's the problem, especially if they don't seem to be getting much thanks for all their efforts. You may also feel a little ratty, particularly if a certain person is criticizing you about something or your workload is so heavy it's interfering with your social life.

• *Tuesday 22 July* •

If something is on your mind at the moment, try to talk it through with a trusted friend or partner today. You'll feel so much better if you can discuss it in detail with someone, because that will help you to sort out your ideas and find out exactly what you think. If a certain person keeps doing things that annoy you, have a gentle chat to them about it now and see if you can improve the situation.

• *Wednesday 23 July* •

Team work will feel really good during the coming four weeks. You'll thoroughly enjoy being with other people and feeling that you're all on the same side, even if this is only a temporary state of affairs. This will definitely be a good opportunity to work with others, rather than against them, so try to concentrate on what unites you with other people instead of what separates you.

• *Thursday 24 July* •

This is a super day for your social life and it may even turn out to be one of the nicest days in the whole of July. Don't be surprised if everyone makes a fuss of you or it's obvious how much they like you. You could receive an enticing invitation or be touched to discover that someone has been thinking about you. If you're at the start of a new relationship, things will go really well between you now.

• *Friday 25 July* •

You're in quite a dreamy state today and will love doing things that reflect this. For example, you might want to lose yourself in a creative enterprise that allows you to indulge your imagination, or you may prefer to be deliciously lazy and do as little as possible. You're also a bit of a romantic now and will enjoy whispering some sweet nothings into the ear of you-know-who.

• *Saturday 26 July* •

Someone is full of good ideas today, or so they tell you. They're rather full of themselves, actually, and you may be rather amused by their huge amounts of confidence. That doesn't mean you should discount everything they say, because some of it could be extremely clever or far-sighted. However, you may want to dismiss some of their wilder promises as nothing more than a lot of hot air.

• *Sunday 27 July* •

Roll up your sleeves because it's a day for getting on with lots of work. If something needs tackling, you're keen to get on with it. What's more, you'll approach it with plenty of energy and care because you won't want to have to do it twice. If you haven't had much exercise recently, this is a good opportunity to make amends. Visit the gym, go for a swim, or find some other way of working up a sweat.

• *Monday 28 July* •

Someone is delightfully considerate today and they seem to have your best interests at heart. They may want to look after you in some way, perhaps by feeding you or taking care of you if you aren't feeling too good. If you're supposed to be watching your weight or steering clear of excess calories at the moment, you'll have your work cut out for you today because you'll find it almost impossible to resist temptation.

● *Tuesday 29 July* ●

If a relationship has been in the doldrums recently, do your best to revitalize it over the next few weeks. Rather than expecting a quick fix, this may involve examining what has gone wrong and acknowledging the part you have played in the situation. You might even have to eat some humble pie but at least this will mean you can get things back on track. What a relief!

● *Wednesday 30 July* ●

Between now and early October, try to devote a lot of thought to your intimate relationships and the resources that you share with other people. For instance, this might be a good opportunity to check that everything is running smoothly in a joint account, and to sort out the problem if it isn't. It will also be a good chance to think about the financial provisions you have made for your future, such as a pension or savings scheme.

● *Thursday 31 July* ●

A certain person indulges in some shock tactics that leave you reeling today. Or maybe it's the other way round and you're the one who drops the bombshell? Either way, the results will take everyone by surprise. There could also be a drama over a financial matter, perhaps when you're presented with an expense that you weren't expecting or discover that there isn't as much money in the bank as you thought.

AUGUST AT A GLANCE

Love	❤ ❤ ❤ ❤ ❤
Money	£ $
Career	💻 💻 💻
Health	☼ ☼

• *Friday 1 August* •

Things really get to you today! You're feeling things much more intensely than usual, which means that someone could get under your skin in no time at all or you might soon start to feel het up about something. There could also be problems with a partner or friend, especially if someone is feeling a little jealous or left out. Navigate your way through these tricky waters with care.

• *Saturday 2 August* •

You're in a much sunnier mood today than you were yesterday, thank goodness, and are able to take things in your stride. It's a super day for being with people who always make you laugh or who take you out of yourself in some way. If you don't have anything planned for the weekend, you could be tempted to take off for a short break, especially if you visit somewhere for the first time.

• *Sunday 3 August* •

This is another day when you love the thought of spreading your wings and doing something different for a change. If you're on unfamiliar territory you'll enjoy going exploring and might even have an adventure along the way. Wherever you are right now, you might decide to visit somewhere that's steeped in history or culture, and which gives you something interesting to think about.

• *Monday 4 August* •

You're caught up in a fog of indecision today, blurring your vision and making it very hard to know what to do next. This could be because you're unsure of how to play it when a certain person is around, or perhaps you've got doubts about the future of your relationship. Alternatively, you may be disorientated because someone is confusing you or filling your head with doubts about yourself.

• *Tuesday 5 August* •

Someone is hard to handle today. They could be in a filthy temper, so you feel you have to pussyfoot around them, or they may be issuing orders left, right and centre. You probably long to tell them where to get off but there may be reasons why you can't do this, such as the fact that this annoying person is your boss or an older relative. However, you may reach a point where you definitely have to say something.

• *Wednesday 6 August* •

Take care today, especially if you're at work or looking after someone who is ill, because it will be almost impossible to stop yourself saying hurtful or rude things in the heat of the moment. You're feeling rather agitated and it won't take much to make you speak out of turn. If you're trying to keep some-thing a secret, you could get so het up now that you blurt out the very thing you were trying to keep quiet.

• *Thursday 7 August* •

Should you give someone the benefit of the doubt or does that make you a soft touch? It's difficult to know today because the situation isn't very clear-cut. What's more, you're eager to behave in ways that won't rock the boat or turn someone against you, even if these aren't in your own best interests. Perhaps your best option is to suspend judgement until you're more sure of yourself?

• *Friday 8 August* •

Friends are tremendous company today and you'll really enjoy being with them. They'll help you to see things in a more positive light if you've been feeling a bit down lately, and you may even be able to laugh at yourself. If you fancy some light relief, get involved in a favourite hobby or take yourself off to a group activity in which you can mix with some kindred spirits.

• *Saturday 9 August* •

This is a wonderful day for talking about whatever is on your mind at the moment, especially if it isn't something you can discuss with just anyone. Even if it feels like a taboo subject, it will do you good now to talk about it with someone you can trust. They may help you to put things into their proper perspective, and you'll feel as though a weight has rolled off your shoulders.

• *Sunday 10 August* •

If you've been having problems with a certain person recently, this is your chance to sort things out between you. Ideally, you should sit them down and talk things through in detail. Don't be afraid to get down to the nitty-gritty of the problem, because that is your best chance of resolving it. Although you'll want to give your side of the story, don't forget to let the other person have their say, too.

• Monday 11 August •

You're in a very compassionate and dreamy mood today, and if possible you won't want the real world to intrude in any way. That means it isn't a very good day for dealing with anything complicated, challenging or detailed because it will be difficult to keep your mind on the job. Instead, you'll excel when using your imagination or tuning in to your intuition.

• Tuesday 12 August •

Today's Full Moon is urging you to take yourself in hand during the coming fortnight. If you want to improve yourself in some way, such as going on a diet or giving up a bad habit, now is the time to swing into action. It's also a super chance to cut out all the dead wood from your life so some fresh growth can follow in due course. Some of this may be painful or poignant, but it will be worth it in the end.

• Wednesday 13 August •

You've very industrious and efficient today, and you are determined to get things done. In fact, nothing is going to stand in your way if you can possibly help it! If you're currently battling your way towards a deadline or you're coping with a heavy schedule, you'll manage to make a lot of progress now. If you need to sort out a financial matter, get cracking on it pronto.

• Thursday 14 August •

Is someone being a bit possessive? It certainly seems that way. You might have to cope with a friend who's miffed because they can't see you when they want to, and who implies that you should put them first. There could also be a little dust-up between you and a certain someone over money, especially if one of you is feeling flush and the other one doesn't like that.

• *Friday 15 August* •

You're in a talkative mood today and you'll enjoy catching up on all the gossip with whoever happens to be around. It will do you good to mix with neighbours or close relatives now, because you'll like being with people who you see on a regular basis. If you can spare the time, how about curling up with a good book or the newspaper and having a nice read?

• *Saturday 16 August* •

Listen to your gut instincts today, particularly when you're with other people. Your intuition may tell you what to talk about or when to back off from certain subjects. If you get the urge to phone someone or write them a letter, act on it because there may be a reason for it that you don't yet know about. At some point, it will do you good to put your feet up and be as lazy as possible. What bliss!

• *Sunday 17 August* •

It's remarkably easy to get on well with other people today, even if they aren't always as amenable as they are right now. What's got into them? Or do you just currently have a knack for keeping them sweet? You're certainly being very diplomatic and polite, and you're also eager to keep things on an even keel. If you need to resolve a problem with someone, this is a very good day to do so.

• *Monday 18 August* •

A partner barely draws breath today because they have so much to talk about. They may even have a tendency to hog the conversation so you can barely get a word in edgeways. Will you mind? You might after a while, especially if you have things that you want to talk about, so do your best to steer the chat in your direction. Unless you do, you'll feel frustrated and annoyed.

• *Tuesday 19 August* •

You're going through a very sociable phase at the moment, and this is another day when you'll enjoy talking to whoever happens to be around. It's an especially good day for getting together with neighbours and other people who you see almost daily. You might want to do this by asking someone in for a drink, or simply by talking to them when you bump into them in the street.

• *Wednesday 20 August* •

Oh dear, there's a lot of friction between you and a certain someone today, and it won't be very pleasant. Maybe you keep rubbing each other up the wrong way, whether intentionally or accidentally, or you have a genuine grievance that is driving a wedge between you. Do your best to sort things out now before they become even more strained. If that means having a row, then so be it.

• *Thursday 21 August* •

This is a super day for being with other people because you're in such a jolly, gregarious mood. It's a wonderful day for being with that special person in your life, especially if you've got something to celebrate. Even if you haven't, you can probably think of something, such as the fact that it's Thursday! What's more, a certain person might make your day, if not your entire month. Fantastic!

• *Friday 22 August* •

The coming three weeks will be a fabulous chance to get a little closer to some of the people in your life. You'll be feeling very seductive, so will enjoy devoting a lot of time to an intimate relationship. But this will also be a good opportunity to establish a greater emotional rapport with other people, especially if you can be honest about your feelings and talk about subjects that are usually off limits for some reason.

• *Saturday 23 August* •

Money has an alarming habit of disappearing at an incredible rate today, so take care if you're going shopping. You might indulge in plenty of impulse buys, which means you end up spending a lot more money than you realize. Alternatively, if you share a bank account with someone, they might be the one who's busy being free with the cash. You might also have an unexpected expense to contend with.

• *Sunday 24 August* •

If you're a typical Aquarian, you can't stand the thought of being tied down by anyone. So it will really get your goat today if someone is being possessive or wants to know your every move whenever you're out of their sight. You may also feel rather oppressed if you spend too much time with other people now, and as though you're living in a hot-house atmosphere from which you need to escape. Try not to say or do anything that is unnecessarily hurtful, though.

• *Monday 25 August* •

This is a good day for being with a partner. It's also super for taking part in any sort of team work because you'll enjoy feeling involved in what's going on. In contrast to yesterday, you'll feel left out if you have to spend too much time by yourself. You may even welcome the opportunity to talk about what happened with someone who is sympathetic but objective.

• *Tuesday 26 August* •

If the problems that blighted you at the weekend haven't yet been sorted out, they will come back to haunt you today. You could easily lose your temper and end up having a rip-roaring row with a certain person, especially if this person is your other half. Mind you, this could be quite exciting and it might end with you hurling yourselves into each other's arms.

• *Wednesday 27 August* •

Things are pretty turbulent with close partners at the moment but take heart because the situation will improve over the next few months. In fact, it's about to get better very soon, thanks to today's New Moon. The coming months will also be an excellent opportunity to salt away some spare cash for a rainy day, or to buy something that will be a huge investment for the future.

• *Thursday 28 August* •

Take care when handling anything connected with your official finances during the next three weeks because things could easily go wrong. You might find that you've filled in a form incorrectly, or that there's a muddle with your credit card company. So check that everything is as it should be, and try to postpone signing any important documents or agreements until 20 September.

• *Friday 29 August* •

This is a really good day for talking through your differences with an intimate partner, because you're in the mood to get things back on track. You don't want this uncomfortable atmosphere to last any longer than necessary. When you do start talking, do your best to speak the truth and to be honest with yourself about your motives and needs. Otherwise, it will all be a waste of time.

• *Saturday 30 August* •

If you really want to improve the situation with you-know-who, you'll be capable of making great strides forward with them today. Between the two of you, you may even reach some radical decisions. If you're currently fancy-free, you might meet someone today who completely bowls you over, especially if they aren't your usual type at all.

• *Sunday 31 August* •

If you're at work today, you'll enjoy getting on with things and doing the best job you can. You might also benefit from the advice of someone who has more experience than you. This is also a good day for considering some of your priorities in life, particularly if they are connected in some way to your ambitions or long-term goals.

SEPTEMBER AT A GLANCE

Love	♥ ♥ ♥
Money	£ $ £ $ £
Career	💻 💻
Health	☼ ☼

• *Monday 1 September* •

This is a super day for getting things done, and you won't want to hang around. It's a great day for demonstrating some of your many talents, particularly if you want to impress someone in authority. This is also an excellent day for getting to grips with official finances, such as making sure that everything is in order or asking someone for their expert opinion.

• *Tuesday 2 September* •

Certain people seem determined to keep you on your toes today. They're keeping you guessing or doing things that mean they're always one step ahead of you, so you feel you're struggling to keep abreast of what's going on. For instance, they might glibly make an announcement that knocks you for six or ask you questions to which you don't know the answers even though you feel you should.

• *Wednesday 3 September* •

You're in a very businesslike mood today, particularly when it comes to getting on with your job. You want to show yourself in as favourable a light as possible, but purely on the basis of your own merits. For instance, if you do something well then you'll want to be praised for it, but you won't expect to be patted on the back just for the sake of it or because your ego needs massaging. If someone pays you a compliment you'll want to know that you deserved it.

• *Thursday 4 September* •

Someone's emotions are near the surface today, making them hot-headed and liable to speak out of turn. They may also lack their usual objectivity, so they get all hot and bothered about something silly or take everything far too personally. If you want an easy, stress-free day, you'd better keep friends and money as far apart as possible, as they'll be a very combustible mixture.

• *Friday 5 September* •

This is another day when love and money could cause endless trouble, so take care. Unfortunately, that won't deter certain people. For example, someone may still be determined to press ahead with their financial demands or to ask you to do them a favour and then get all huffy when you politely refuse. There could also be some bad feeling when someone tries to exert their emotional freedom. A tricky day.

• *Saturday 6 September* •

After the difficulties of the past two days, you're in need of some solace. Luckily, it arrives in the shape of a certain person who will soon make you feel better. They might encourage you to pour out your heart to them while they listen sympathetically, or they might do something nice that soon makes you forget about your troubles. There could also be lots of romance in the air now. Great!

• *Sunday 7 September* •

You're full of enthusiasm today and are eager to push yourself further than usual. For instance, if you're out shopping you will want to spend more money than you can comfortably afford or might be prepared to take a gamble on something. You also fancy trying your luck when it comes to matters of the heart, and if you're currently in hot pursuit of someone you'll go all out to win them now. Good luck!

• *Monday 8 September* •

If financial matters have ruffled a few feathers recently, this is a great opportunity to put things to rights. Right now you've got the ability to sweet-talk almost anyone out of their sulks, so don't waste this chance to charm them into submission.

However, it's important that you avoid any tendency to appear insincere because that will soon sound a false note and won't improve the situation at all.

• *Tuesday 9 September* •

You fancy a little retail excitement today, so watch out if you're going past the shops. It's one of those days when you want to buy things just for the sake of it, so you may even decide to splash out on something that you don't even want or like very much. You could also have temporary second thoughts about something or someone that has always been important to you. But, right now, you aren't so sure.

• *Wednesday 10 September* •

Today's Full Moon is sounding a note of caution about your current financial state. If you've been spending money like water recently, perhaps it's time to start telling yourself that there's a drought! Even if you don't go on a strict economy drive, you should think seriously about your outgoings and decide whether it's time to cut back on some of your expenses. Maybe the money is better spent elsewhere?

• *Thursday 11 September* •

A certain person is quite voluble today, as you'll soon discover. They're especially chatty when it comes to talking about subjects that are usually off limits for some reason. You may be embarrassed at first, but you'll soon realize that it's liberating to discuss topics that are normally considered taboo, such as death or sex.

• *Friday 12 September* •

You're in a very easy-going mood today and will enjoy being with people who are gentle and sensitive. They may show you a lot of consideration or affection, or perhaps it will be the other way round. It's a particularly good day for talking to neighbours or close relatives, even if you have a desultory chat about nothing in particular. It's being in each other's company that counts now.

• *Saturday 13 September* •

You're in the mood to straighten things out and put matters to rights today. For instance, you might decide that this is your chance to sort out a problem with a certain person by discussing it with them in a lot of detail. It's also a good day to check that household appliances and gadgets are behaving themselves. If you think something is about to go on the blink, perhaps you should get it serviced before it lets you down just when you need it most.

• *Sunday 14 September* •

Finances are never far from your thoughts today, especially if you want to sort out a money problem. You may not be able to do much about it until tomorrow but you'll still want to organize your plan of campaign now. If you're considering some domestic expenses, it's a good day for working out a budget or deciding whether your ideas are feasible.

• *Monday 15 September* •

During the next few weeks you'll really enjoy getting involved with things and people that are outside your usual orbit. For instance, if you're about to go on holiday you'll love exploring your new surroundings and you might even lose your heart in the process. Whether you're staying put or about to go off on your travels, you'll fall in love with all that life has to offer. The more you throw yourself into the experience, the more you'll get in return.

• *Tuesday 16 September* •

Sort out your domestic finances today, particularly if that means going through your expenses or checking that the adults in the household are paying their way. If you're doing some food shopping you'll be keen to track down some bargains but you won't want to compromise on quality. It's also a super day for being with loved ones.

• *Wednesday 17 September* •

Someone is in a very generous mood today, whether they give their time, affection or money. They might make a fuss of you, pay you a compliment or make you laugh about something. If you've been with your other half longer than you care to remember, you'll be reminded all over again about why you chose to be with them in the first place.

• *Thursday 18 September* •

There's a lot of emotional tension in the air, and it's almost bound to make the sparks fly sooner or later. Actually, it will be much better to get things out into the open, even if that means having a shouting match, than to bottle them up and then seethe with resentment for the rest of the day. So if you're angry about something, get it off your chest before you reach screaming point.

• *Friday 19 September* •

Work and pleasure don't mix today. For example, you may have to put in extra hours over some chores and forgo something that you were looking forward to. Alternatively, a colleague may not be very friendly or they might make a fuss about something. If you're on holiday, be careful about what you eat because you could be susceptible to stomach troubles.

• *Saturday 20 September* •

If you've sensibly been holding back on making big decisions about your finances recently, you can get things moving again from today. You may even discover that, in the interim, you've changed your mind about something that is still up in the air so you're glad that you didn't act on it before now. If you've been in dispute with a partner recently, they may start to change their tune over the next few days.

• *Sunday 21 September* •

This is a super day for working in tandem with other people. Any form of team work is better now than going your own way, and you'll really enjoy the sense of belonging to a gang of people, even if it's only on a temporary basis. Although this won't be why you're doing it, there could be the added bonus of a perk or an extra payment.

• *Monday 22 September* •

It will be almost impossible to get a straight answer out of you-know-who today, so you may not even bother to try. They may be hiding something, sitting on the fence, or simply off on another planet. However, before you start laying the blame on their shoulders, you should realize that you may also give the impression that you're rather flaky or distracted right now. Is something bothering you?

• *Tuesday 23 September* •

Between now and this time next month you'll be in a very adventurous mood. You'll jump at the chance to seize an opportunity or accept a challenge, even if it's something that seems very ambitious or beyond your grasp. This will also be a fabulous opportunity to widen your horizons in some way, whether you do it through travel or knowledge.

• Wednesday 24 September •

You're drawn to someone who's gentle and sensitive today. They may even have an other-worldly quality which you will find very attractive. They might also be in contact with elusive or mystical realms, or radiate a spiritual energy. This will all be very seductive and you will probably want to know more. If you meet them for the first time now, you'll always regard them as someone special.

• Thursday 25 September •

Take care because your feelings are easily hurt now. You could be cut to the quick by someone's implied or direct criticism of you, especially if you suspect that they are disappointed in you for some reason. There could be an ethical or moral element to all this, perhaps with you out of favour for transgressing in some way. Are you taking things too seriously or is this person being too strict? Or is it a bit of both?

• Friday 26 September •

The coming fortnight promises to be really exciting, with some fabulous opportunities about to appear over the horizon. If you're really lucky you could get the chance to do something that you've always wanted, or be able to spread your wings and take off in a new direction. But don't wait for things to land in your lap because to a large extent you'll make your own luck now.

• Saturday 27 September •

Life is pretty lively today, and that's exactly the way you want it to be. You're in the mood for some excitement, especially if it means that you won't know what's going to happen next. This is a great day for planning future activities, so you've got something to look forward to. It's also good for keeping an open mind about things – you could learn something very interesting as a result.

• *Sunday 28 September* •

Someone is in a very inquisitive mood today and they won't rest until they've got to the bottom of any mysteries or puzzles that are currently bothering them. Unfortunately, this will feel a bit like the third degree if you're on the receiving end of it because they won't relax until they've got all the answers to their questions. In the meantime, they may be unduly suspicious of you.

• *Monday 29 September* •

You'll get the chance to draw closer to a friend today and to establish a greater sense of intimacy with them. This will be especially likely if you're able to share a secret or you discuss a topic that has a lot of meaning for both of you. If you meet someone for the first time today you'll be intrigued by each other and will want to know more. It could be the start of a fascinating relationship.

• *Tuesday 30 September* •

You're in a lively and outgoing mood today, which means you won't want to spend any time alone if you can possibly help it. This is a terrific day for making contact with friends and acquaintances, especially if you haven't seen each other for a while. You'll also enjoy taking part in a group activity, but don't be surprised if you're asked to become more involved in it than you are at the moment.

OCTOBER AT A GLANCE

Love	♥ ♥ ♥
Money	£ $ £
Career	💻 💻 💻 💻 💻
Health	☼ ☼

• *Wednesday 1 October* •

You're in an outgoing and friendly mood today, making it a very sociable start to October. It's one of those days when you'll feel much happier if you're with other people than if you're left to your own devices. Once again, you'll enjoy being with people who are on the same wavelength as you, especially if you have some interests in common or they feel like kindred spirits.

• *Thursday 2 October* •

Oh dear! It looks like being a tricky day, with some form of conflict between openness and secrecy. Maybe you want to be honest about something but you feel you should keep quiet about it, or perhaps a secret is about to get an airing against your wishes. There could also be problems if someone mentions a belief or philosophy that is dear to their heart because it might clash with someone else's ideas. It seems that discretion is the better part of valour right now.

• *Friday 3 October* •

Look after yourself today because it won't take much to make you feel down in the dumps or exhausted. If you're facing a pile of work, the very thought of it will be enough to make you want to go back to bed. Try to steer clear of anyone who's a human germ factory because you'll be very susceptible to their bugs now. It won't help if something is preying on your mind or keeping you awake at night. Isn't there something constructive you can do about it?

• *Saturday 4 October* •

You're very open-minded today and want to understand more about the world. You might be drawn to a religion or spiritual practice that offers you a chance to connect with something greater than yourself, or you may simply want to show unconditional love to everyone you meet now. You might even feel that you are changing in some subtle but fundamental way.

• *Sunday 5 October* •

This is a super day for getting on well with everyone you come across. You aren't interested in divisions caused by race, creed, class or gender, because you want to rise above such things. You could have a fascinating conversation with someone that encourages you to view the world in a different way. It's also a fabulous chance to expand your knowledge, whether formally or informally.

• *Monday 6 October* •

It feels as though you've got your nose glued to the grindstone today. Maybe you're labouring under a huge pile of work and it's getting you down, or perhaps you've got to please someone who has very high standards that are almost impossible to meet. You may also be listening to the voice of your conscience, which is busy ticking you off about something and making you feel uncomfortable. What a day!

• *Tuesday 7 October* •

Keep your mind and your options open if you want to make the most of the next three weeks. This will be a wonderful chance to add to your store of knowledge in some way because you'll have so much curiosity about everything. You might find it hard to prise a fascinating book out of your hands, or you may be gripped by some documentaries on television. Anything that makes you think is good now.

• *Wednesday 8 October* •

Prepare yourself for what could be a frustrating day, when things don't go the way you want or people aren't around when you need them. Communications could also go haywire now, perhaps when your phone goes on the blink or your mobile's battery runs down at the very moment when you need it most. If you arrange an appointment today it may have to be altered or even cancelled at a later date.

• *Thursday 9 October* •

You're dazzled and attracted by someone's personality today. The more unusual or unconventional they are, the stronger the chemistry between you now. This will be rather exciting, because it will open your mind to all sorts of possibilities or ideas that have never occurred to you before. If you're given the opportunity to do some travelling now, you'll want to jump at it.

• *Friday 10 October* •

The Full Moon today will influence your communications during the next two weeks. This might mean that you end up having a serious discussion with someone in which you're able to say things that have been on your mind for a long time.

It will also be a good opportunity to sort out any problems with a neighbour or close relative, particularly if you want to put the whole episode behind you.

• *Saturday 11 October* •

Life is full of exciting possibilities at the moment, and some more occur to you today. One of these ideas may even have a galvanizing effect on one of your plans for the future, perhaps because it shows how you can turn something from a pipe dream into reality. You may also get the chance to change a friend's mind gently about something that they mistakenly think is true.

• *Sunday 12 October* •

It's one of those days when you want to take a back seat and let life carry on without you. Maybe you don't have as much energy as usual, or you're feeling worn down by adverse circumstances and need to recharge your batteries. Be careful if you're with other people because they may put you on the defensive, possibly without even knowing what they're doing. Perhaps you're being too sensitive for your own good?

• *Monday 13 October* •

You're captivated by mysteries today and will love getting engrossed in anything that seems to ask more questions than it answers. For instance, you might have a conversation about ghosts and then want to find out more about them. Telling your own fortune could also appeal to you now, so you could be inspired to get out your tarot cards and see what fate has in store for you.

• *Tuesday 14 October* •

Someone is a very hard taskmaster today. They might treat you to a great big dose of criticism, or give the impression that you're letting the side down in some way. Do they have a point or are they being far too strict? If you're currently trying to meet a deadline or stick to a schedule, you'll feel guilty if you don't devote every possible minute to the task. But you can't work round the clock, can you?

• *Wednesday 15 October* •

Enjoy yourself because this is one of those glorious days when things go according to plan and it's easy to hit it off with everyone you meet. You're in a very sunny-tempered mood and are happy to make an effort to get on the right side of others. There could also be a light-hearted flirtation between you and a certain person – or perhaps you mean every word of it?

• *Thursday 16 October* •

You're in the mood to roll up your sleeves and get on with whatever needs to be tackled today. You'd much rather tick it off your list of things to do than put it to one side and then have to worry about it. Try to get some exercise at some point because you'll enjoy being active. If you don't fancy a visit to the gym, jog round the block instead or do some energetic housework.

• *Friday 17 October* •

This is a really good day for talking to friends and acquaintances, especially if you want to have an in-depth discussion with them. You'll also enjoy giving your brain a good workout by having an intellectual conversation. If you've been puzzled by a mystery recently, this is a great day to get to the bottom of it or at least to get a glimmer of what's going on.

• *Saturday 18 October* •

Someone has some rather unrealistic ideas today, and these could soon lead to disappointment. For instance, you might discover that a certain person is not who you think they are, perhaps because they fail to behave in the way you imagined they would. What's going on here? Has this person let you down by not doing what you expected, or have you placed them on an impossibly high pedestal?

• *Sunday 19 October* •

A woman needs careful handling today. She may need a lot of attention or praise, otherwise she might complain or stage a scene. It's nothing to worry about but nevertheless it is something to be aware of. There could also be a minor sense of rivalry between two people, perhaps because they're competing for someone's affection or they both want to be in the limelight.

• *Monday 20 October* •

It may be Monday but you're very happy to get on with your work now. In fact, you'll take pride in what you achieve, especially if you're working as part of a team. This is a day when you'll all pull together, giving each other moral support and encouragement. This is also a good day for building up a strong rapport with someone you respect or admire. They may act as a mentor to you in some way.

• *Tuesday 21 October* •

You're very keen to understand other people's opinions today, even if you don't agree with everything they say. Instead of rigidly sticking to your own viewpoint and refusing to accept anything that contradicts it, you're eager to listen to other people's perspectives. You may even be so open-minded that you're happy to revise your thoughts in view of what you are told now.

• *Wednesday 22 October* •

You're on the hunt for adventure and mental stimulation today, and will welcome any events that promise to make life interesting. You might decide to do something daring or challenging on the spur of the moment, just to see if you can do it. You could also be strongly attracted by something that seems unconventional by other people's standards but which is right up your street at the moment.

• *Thursday 23 October* •

You've been keen to expand your horizons recently but the picture changes from today, making you more interested in focusing on your goals and ambitions during the next four weeks. There will even be times when you feel that your identity is completely bound up in what you have achieved and how other people regard you, so your reputation and social status will have extra importance for you now.

• *Friday 24 October* •

The next few weeks are a fantastic chance to think about ways to make more progress in the world. If you think you're lacking in qualifications or skills, this is a super opportunity to add to your existing talents by learning something new. You might even decide that you're going to retrain for a new job or profession because you're so fed up with what you're doing at the moment.

• *Saturday 25 October* •

Today's New Moon emphasizes all the ideas that have occurred to you during the past couple of days and urges you to do something concrete about them. Use the energy of this New Moon to set the ball rolling and get some of your plans off the ground. It will also herald a very rewarding phase in your relationship with someone who is older, wiser or more powerful than you, and who can teach you a great deal.

• *Sunday 26 October* •

Want to make friends and influence people? Well, you shouldn't have any problems on that score today because you'll give a good impression to everyone you meet. If you're at work, you'll take pride in doing things to the best of your ability. You might also have a very useful conversation with a certain person, in which you are able to get them on your side.

• *Monday 27 October* •

If you're a typical Aquarian you can't stand the feeling of being stuck in a mindless routine. So you'll find life difficult today, when things feel stale or boring. If you're working, you'll want to liven things up as soon as they threaten to become predictable. However, that could cause endless ructions or backfire on you in some way, so be careful how you go about it.

• *Tuesday 28 October* •

You're skilled at standing up for yourself if necessary today, so you'll know what to say if you're hauled over the coals for what happened yesterday. It's a great day if you're taking part in a meeting or discussion because you'll have no qualms about defending your opinions and sticking to your guns. However, don't fall into the trap of thinking that you're right and anyone who disagrees with you must be wrong.

• *Wednesday 29 October* •

This is an excellent day for getting on with whatever needs to be done, although you'll make the most progress if you can be left to your own devices. You'll prefer it this way because it will be easier to concentrate without any distractions from other people. You may also be reluctant to share the limelight with others, or be worried that any praise will go to them instead of you.

• *Thursday 30 October* •

Someone who is supposed to know what they're talking about appears to be having a brainstorm today. They may say something that sounds like absolute nonsense to you, or they might keep contradicting themselves. Be careful if you're giving someone orders or instructions because these may not be very clear and might result in a complete muddle that takes ages to sort out. So make sure you mean what you say, and don't leave any room for doubt!

• *Friday 31 October* •

You'll really appreciate someone's knowledge or understanding today, especially if you find yourself confiding in them about something. This is certainly a good day for pouring your heart out to someone because you'll feel so much better for it. Alternatively, you may be the one who's operating in an advisory capacity and who is dishing out the tea and sympathy.

NOVEMBER AT A GLANCE

Love	❤ ❤
Money	£ $
Career	💻 💻 💻 💻 💻
Health	☼ ☼

• *Saturday 1 November* •

Is someone being very bossy today? It certainly seems that way because they're so busy issuing orders and making you run around after them. Or are you being very huffy and quick to take offence? It will be difficult to know because you're in such a subjective mood and this other person is being rather forceful. You may be tempted to have it out with them, and that would certainly be better than feeling resentful and letting the tension build between you.

• *Sunday 2 November* •

You have a burning desire to shock someone today. The more upright, conventional or hidebound they seem, the more you'll want to take them by surprise or pull the rug out from under them. Although this may fill you with satisfaction at the time it could easily cause trouble for you in the long run, perhaps because you've stepped out of line or ruffled too many feathers. Can't you let off steam in less controversial ways?

• *Monday 3 November* •

If you transgressed yesterday, someone will do their utmost to make you feel bad about it today. They could rub your nose in it and keep reminding you of how you did something wrong, or they might be all high and mighty and morally superior. Be careful if you're with someone who likes to bolster their own ego at the expense of others because they might easily do just that to you right now.

• Tuesday 4 November •

This is a good day for getting on with anything connected with red tape or officialdom. For instance, you might be inspired to fill in some forms or to complete a complicated questionnaire. If you're trying to sort out a financial matter connected with your job, such as a question about your pay, this is a great day to find out what's going on or to jog someone's memory about it.

• Wednesday 5 November •

You're in a businesslike mood today and want to tuck a lot under your belt. Actually, you're both efficient and practical now, so you'll make a fabulous impression on anyone who happens to be watching you at the moment. If you're going to a job interview you'll have little to worry about because you'll give such a good impression. Alternatively, you might be offered a promotion or bonus in your current workplace.

• Thursday 6 November •

People are very co-operative and helpful today, especially if you ask their advice or want to pick their brains about something. You'll also be generous with your knowledge, given half the chance. An opportunity could come your way, courtesy of someone who has more clout or experience than you, and you'll jump at it, especially if money is involved.

• Friday 7 November •

Do your best to get out and about as much as possible today because you never know who you might bump into in the process. You could meet the very person you wanted to see, or come across someone who's been a bit of a stranger recently. Keep your ears pinned back because you might hear of an interesting coincidence or a surprising piece of gossip.

• *Saturday 8 November* •

You're feeling pragmatic today, which makes it a great day for taking things in your stride. You'll do your best to remain calm and unruffled, and will quietly go about whatever needs to be done. This is a good chance to get on with some of the chores, even if they aren't very exciting. You'll be pleased to get them out of the way. You may also take something to be repaired.

• *Sunday 9 November* •

The coming fortnight will be very significant for you because it's a chance to make some important decisions about your home and family life. These may not be very easy and they could also stir up some poignant emotions, but you'll know that they have to be faced. There is also a chance that you may have to come to terms with something or someone from your past, and to accept that what's done is done.

• *Monday 10 November* •

You aren't feeling very patient or understanding today, as you will quickly demonstrate if someone gets on your nerves. You'll be particularly irritated by people who seem very meek or who are frightened to say boo to a goose. You'll either want to encourage them to stand up for themselves or you'll be tempted to do something that makes them jump out of their skin.

• *Tuesday 11 November* •

Someone has some radical ideas today. The question is whether these are any good or not. Do your best to keep an open mind about them, especially if they are really challenging, and don't fall into the trap of dismissing them without another thought. You should also beware of treating them like the emperor's new clothes and thinking that they must be very clever or radical simply because you can't make head nor tail of them. Sounds as though you'll have to do some mental gymnastics!

• *Wednesday 12 November* •

The rest of November will be a super opportunity to think about your hopes and dreams for the future. If you haven't made much progress with them lately, it's time to dust them off and reassess them in the light of what you now know. You may want to put some of them in mothballs but others could be really inspiring and exciting. You may also want to start making some New Year resolutions for 2004.

• *Thursday 13 November* •

You're blessed with abundant energy today, and you want to put it to good use whenever you get the chance. That might mean dashing around hither and thither, busily getting things done. Or it could send you straight round to the gym or leisure centre. If you're at work, you'll want to take charge of things whenever it is appropriate and to show that you know what you're doing.

• *Friday 14 November* •

This is a terrific day for getting on with whatever is top of your list of priorities. Even if you've been putting it off lately, you now want to tackle it and get it out of the way. You'll take a lot of care over things now because you want to do them properly, and you certainly don't want to waste your time by having to do something twice because you didn't get it right first time round.

• *Saturday 15 November* •

Feeling extravagant? It's more than likely today because you're in the mood to spend money and you don't care about the expense. If you see something you like you'll want to cast financial caution to the winds, which could be rather risky if you're currently feeling strapped for cash. Yet you're in no mood to stint yourself, either financially or emotionally. Instead, you want to be as hedonistic as possible.

• *Sunday 16 November* •

A partner could easily get the wrong end of the stick today and cause a lot of confusion before you're able to sort things out. Or maybe you're the one who's in a bit of a fog and who is misreading the situation? You're in a highly sensitive mood, which will make you very susceptible to the emotional undercurrents swirling around you. Try not to make mountains out of molehills as a result.

• *Monday 17 November* •

If the tension has been building up between you and a certain person recently, it will come to a head today. There could be a showdown or a big row, but although this won't be very pleasant at the time at least it will be a chance to clear the air. However, do your best not to say more than you intended, nor to drag in past resentments that have nothing to do with the current problem.

• *Tuesday 18 November* •

A friend exudes emotional intensity today, and being with them will be a very powerful experience. You might have an in-depth conversation which helps you to understand one another as never before, or which alters your relationship in some way. If you've been wondering if you're attracted to a chum, what transpires between you now will leave you in no doubt about the state of your heart.

• *Wednesday 19 November* •

It's a good day for talking to other people because you'll find it so easy to get on their wavelength. This could happen even if you're with someone who you don't know very well. Your gut instincts might be working overtime where a certain person is concerned, in which case you should listen carefully to your intuition and act accordingly. For instance, you might get the urge to phone them and then discover that they were about to call you, or that they need your help.

• *Thursday 20 November* •

Financial prudence flies straight out of the window today because you can't be bothered with it. Instead, you want to do something daring or risky. Whether or not this is a good idea depends on how cautious you usually are. If you're normally almost too conservative for words, you might now do something that works out well. But if you're already rash with your cash, you might now behave in ways that are very foolish or reckless.

• *Friday 21 November* •

Any hint of restrictions or obstructions will be like a red rag to a bull today, making you want to put your head down and steamroller your way through them. This is especially likely if you're presented with rules that are apparently crying out to be broken because they strike you as so arbitrary or senseless. However, be very careful when defying officials or superiors because you might cause a lot of trouble.

• *Saturday 22 November* •

During the next four weeks you'll enjoy taking part in group activities. You will get a kick out of blending in with other people, especially if you share the same ideals or interests. It will feel good to know that you are all on the same side or that you're working towards a common goal. You will also be keen to show people who you really are, and to demonstrate your integrity.

• *Sunday 23 November* •

Friends will have an important impact on your life during the next couple of weeks, thanks to today's eclipsed New Moon. A chum might make a suggestion that sparks off all sorts of brilliant ideas in your mind, or which sets you off on a completely new path. This will also be an excellent chance to widen your circle of friends by joining a group, club or organization that caters for one of your interests.

• *Monday 24 November* •

Someone is rather outspoken today, so don't be surprised if they speak out of turn or say something that puts you on the defensive. They could be especially vociferous when it comes to talking about money or possessions. The atmosphere could quickly get overheated, making you want to join in and have your say as well. It could become a free-for-all before you know it!

• *Tuesday 25 November* •

You're asking some searching questions today and you won't be content until you've got some answers. However, be careful how you go about this because you may make someone feel that they're being grilled. If you're already suspicious about a certain person's behaviour or motives, what happens now is likely to add fuel to the fire. Or are you letting your imagination run away with you?

• *Wednesday 26 November* •

Someone has an iron-clad will today, as they soon demonstrate. If you want them to do something that they aren't happy about, you'll go blue in the face before they change their mind. Is it really worth the effort? Unfortunately, their insistence on sticking to their guns will be matched by your determination to do the same, and the result can only be a big, fat stalemate. So where do you go from here?

• *Thursday 27 November* •

Between now and mid-December you'll value your privacy even more than usual. There may even be times when your idea of heaven is to shut the door on the rest of the world and luxuriate in some peace and quiet. Romance could also be on the agenda now, especially if you don't want to make your relationship public. For instance, you might get involved in an illicit affair in which everything has to be conducted in the greatest secrecy.

• *Friday 28 November* •

This is a super day for mixing with kindred spirits and other people who are on the same wavelength as you. You might want to get together with a gang of friends, or maybe you have one chum in mind. If you're attending a group activity, you might be asked to take a leading role in what's going on, even if you weren't expecting it.

• *Saturday 29 November* •

Once again, this is a day for being with friends and acquaintances. You'll love chatting to them about whatever pops into your heads, so you could have some very wide-ranging conversations. If you haven't yet got round to organizing your Christmas cards, spring into action now. You might even be inspired to write some letters to friends who live far away.

• *Sunday 30 November* •

Is someone's nose out of joint today? It certainly seems that way, judging by their behaviour. For instance, they might be miffed because they haven't seen much of you lately or they could be annoyed if you can't be with them today. There could also be friction over the cost of a social event or the emotional demands that a friend is making on you. Try to sort things out as reasonably as possible.

DECEMBER AT A GLANCE

Love	♥ ♥ ♥ ♥
Money	£ $
Career	💻 💻
Health	☼ ☼ ☼

• *Monday 1 December* •

Whether or not it's the thought of the forthcoming festivities, you're in the mood to spend money today. In fact, you're happy to splash it around in all directions, even if you're currently flat broke. This is the perfect opportunity to make some progress with your Christmas shopping, although you may not bother about looking at price tags or sticking to your lists because you'll buy things as you see them. You may even take a few wild guesses about whether some things will be suitable.

• *Tuesday 2 December* •

There will be times throughout December when you'll want to play your cards close to your chest and not say too much. There may even be occasions when you almost seem to have taken a vow of silence because you'll be so taciturn. Although it might be a good idea to keep quiet at certain moments, you must be careful not to give the impression that you are sulking or that you are indifferent to what is happening around you. That would be asking for trouble!

• *Wednesday 3 December* •

You're in a very compassionate and sensitive mood today, and it will be very easy to tune into the feelings of the people around you. You may even feel that there is no need for words when you're with a certain person. A charity or good cause could appeal to you now, making you wonder how you can lend a hand. You might decide to donate some money or to offer your time instead.

• *Thursday 4 December* •

You're in the mood to get out and about today, and you'll soon start to feel cooped up if you have to spend too long in one place. It will do you good to have a change of scene at some point, even if you can't spare much time there. If you're going shopping, you'll enjoy searching out unusual items and you might even find some witty or clever stocking fillers.

• *Friday 5 December* •

If you aren't careful, a pall of gloom will descend on you today, making you feel fed up and anxious. You may not even be able to put your finger on what's wrong, which means you won't know how to put things right. If you do know what's bugging you, you may dismiss it as something very minor, such as a disturbing dream or the strange mood of a member of the family. Try to stay positive.

• *Saturday 6 December* •

A certain someone is hard to get along with today. They may be one step removed from you, so you are uncomfortably aware of the emotional distance between you. You could also be divided by the fact that one of you isn't feeling very well and is therefore distracted. Duty or work may also drive a wedge between you, but try not to imagine that things are worse than they really are.

• *Sunday 7 December* •

Is it your imagination or is a certain so-and-so going out of their way to cause trouble today? They might stir up a lot of ill feeling with an apparently innocent remark, and then sit back to see what happens next. This is most likely to happen if they get bored or restless, so it may help if you give them plenty to keep them busy. Even so, are you really responsible for their behaviour?

• *Monday 8 December* •

A loved one will give you plenty to think about during the coming fortnight. They might do something that forces you to revise your opinion of them, or say something that makes you see them in a new light. If you've fallen out with a favourite person or there has been a rift between you, this might be your chance to put matters to rights and to kiss and make up. Or perhaps you want to bring the relationship to an end in light of what has happened?

• *Tuesday 9 December* •

It's difficult to keep your emotions under control today and you may decide that it's completely impossible. You might be brooding about what's been taking place with you-know-who, and feel that nothing can ever put it right. Or you could be gripped by jealousy of someone and feel as though it's poisoning the very air you breathe. Try to keep things in proportion while facing up to your emotions.

• *Wednesday 10 December* •

Think twice if someone tries to talk you into joining them in a financial venture today. Everything may sound OK but are you sure it's a safe bet? This person may have got carried away with enthusiasm, so that they're exaggerating the benefits of what they're proposing or have forgotten to mention some of the possible pitfalls. If something sounds as though it's too good to be true then you can be almost certain that it is!

• *Thursday 11 December* •

Your heart swells with affection for some of the people in your life today, putting you in a very generous and demonstrative mood. Or maybe you're only interested in showing your feelings to a certain someone? If you've been suffering from unrequited love and are waiting for your beloved to notice that you exist, they could take you by surprise now and sweep you off your feet. At long last!

• *Friday 12 December* •

Have you thought about your New Year resolutions yet? This is the perfect day to start sketching out your plans because you'll take them very seriously and will do your utmost to turn them into reality. If that means making some adjustments to some of your current ideas then you will be happy to do so. You could also be consumed by an ideal that aims to make the world a better place. But don't ram it down other people's throats if they don't want to know about it.

• *Saturday 13 December* •

It will be horribly easy to let worries eat away at you today until you don't know what to do with yourself. Try to keep things in perspective, and avoid talking to people who are real doom merchants because they will only make you feel worse. If you're anxious about a health matter, promise yourself to do something about it as soon as possible. What is to be gained from getting in a state like this?

• *Sunday 14 December* •

The more socializing you can do today, the more you'll enjoy yourself. You certainly won't want to be left to your own devices if you can avoid it. If you don't have anything planned, how about inviting some people over to your place or arranging to meet them in the pub? You will also enjoy talking to someone who shares one of your interests or hobbies.

• *Monday 15 December* •

Have you finished writing your Christmas cards yet? If not, get them out of the way today if possible. Once you get started, you'll enjoy writing special messages in your cards or even dashing off a few letters. You're in the mood to talk about your feelings and could become involved in a searching conversation with someone in which you both bare your souls. You'll feel so much better for it!

• *Tuesday 16 December* •

You'll have abundant energy during the next few weeks and will enjoy keeping on your toes. Actually, it will be important to stay busy because if you have any periods of enforced inactivity you might quickly start to feel agitated, restless or irritable. If the thought of organizing the forthcoming festivities usually horrifies you, for once you'll want to throw yourself into them and devote lots of time to them.

• *Wednesday 17 December* •

There will be times between now and early January when you'll have to choose your words very carefully. If you don't, you might give someone the wrong impression or imply things that you don't mean. If you're currently working on a project or idea that has to be kept under wraps, it could hit some snags or delays. These will be frustrating but will give you the chance to revise your thinking if necessary.

• *Thursday 18 December* •

Do yourself a favour and keep away from contentious or touchy subjects today. For instance, if someone starts talking about their religion you might decide that it's wise to change the subject and avoid saying the wrong thing. However, there could still be some verbal fisticuffs at some point, despite your best efforts. You may also discover to your horror that a secret has now become exposed to everyone's scrutiny.

• *Friday 19 December* •

You'll enjoy keeping on the go as much as possible today, and it will be great if you have a complete change of scene at some point. It will also be a super day for mixing with people who understand the way you think or who share some of your interests. If you haven't heard from some far-off friends for a while, write them a letter, send them an e-mail or give them a ring. You might even arrange to visit them.

• *Saturday 20 December* •

If something has been worrying you recently, you could find yourself telling someone all about it today. You may not have intended to do this, but somehow it will all come out in the course of the conversation. This will come as a great relief to you because it will help you to organize your thoughts, and you might also benefit from this person's opinion or advice.

• *Sunday 21 December* •

With perfect timing for the approaching festivities, you enter an extremely sociable and easy-going phase from today. During the next few weeks you'll do your utmost to get on well with everyone you meet, sometimes even to the point of reaching compromises that are not in your best interests. Today will also be a wonderful chance to buy yourself some new clothes or improve your appearance in some way.

• *Monday 22 December* •

You're in a very conscientious frame of mind today, making you anxious to do whatever is expected of you. If you're at work and ploughing your way through a pile of things that have to be completed before the holidays begin, you'll drive yourself hard and will put in some overtime if that is the only way to meet your deadlines. You may also be worried about not pulling your weight, even though that seems very unlikely at the moment.

• Tuesday 23 December •

Try to look on the coming fortnight as the chance for a complete rest. You may not be able to put your feet up for the entire period, but do your utmost to set aside some time to yourself every now and then. You might also enjoy some form of contemplation or meditation, especially if you've never tried them before. They could have some very beneficial effects on you, so don't discount them without giving them a try.

• Wednesday 24 December •

You have a generous heart today, and it shows. You might give someone a big hug, tell them how much you love them or do something else that boosts their ego. If you're going to a party or gathering, what starts off as a flirtatious chat with someone could lead to other things.

• Thursday 25 December •

From the moment you wake up, you'll want to fill the day with as much enjoyment and excitement as possible. You'll also go out of your way to make it a super Christmas for everyone else. For instance, you'll want to keep on the right side of everyone, even if some of these people usually drive you round the bend with irritation. You'll be full of sunny smiles right now!

• Friday 26 December •

The atmosphere is rather combustible and tense today, and there may be times when you have to pussyfoot around everyone to avoid explosions. However, despite your best efforts it looks as though there could be a row or showdown at some point, especially if someone lets the cat out of the bag or drops a brick. If you've been seething with resentment about someone or something, it could all come out in a big rush now.

• Saturday 27 December •

You're keen to talk today, and you'll be especially interested in talking about subjects that you usually keep under wraps. For instance, you might tell someone some of your deep dark secrets, or confide in them about something that has been bothering you. It may be a relief to get things off your chest but try to avoid dominating the conversation if the other person also has something to say, and be wary of getting carried away and revealing things that you'll later wish you had kept quiet about.

• Sunday 28 December •

A certain person is very expansive today. They're demonstrative and affectionate, which will be nice, but they may also come on a bit strong. You may even end up wanting to make your excuses and leave. If someone is down on their luck at the moment they might ask you to help them out. Although you'll be glad to do what you can, you won't like it if they try to make you feel obliged to stump up.

• Monday 29 December •

If you want to keep something a secret, don't divulge it to another living soul today. Otherwise your confidences could have a nasty habit of becoming the subject of the latest gossip. Bear this in mind, too, if someone buttonholes you and starts to tell you a secret. If you know you won't be able to keep it to yourself, do your best to dissuade this person from telling you anything more about it.

• *Tuesday 30 December* •

Given half a chance, you'll soon be lost in a world of your own today. You could be feeling very dreamy and romantic, making you want to think only about pleasant subjects that won't disturb your current sense of peace. Today is a wonderful opportunity to explore some of your creative talents because this is where you'll excel. However, you won't do so well when dealing with harsh reality, which will unnerve you.

• *Wednesday 31 December* •

You end the year in a serious and reflective mood. You also have a tendency to concentrate on negative ideas rather than anything positive now, so if you're thinking back over what 2003 brought you, you may forget about some of the nice things that happened. If you're feeling tired, it won't do you any good to soldier on regardless. Give yourself a break!

YOUR AQUARIUS SUN SIGN

In this chapter I am going to tell you all about your Aquarius Sun sign. But what is a Sun sign? It often gets called a star sign, but are they the same thing? Well, yes, although 'Sun sign' is a more accurate term. Your Sun sign is the sign that the Sun occupied when you were born. Every year, the Sun moves through the heavens and spends an average of 30 days in each of the twelve signs. When you were born, the Sun was moving through the sign of Aquarius, so this is your Sun or star sign.

This chapter tells you everything you want to know about your Aquarius Sun sign. To start off, I describe your general personality – what makes you tick. Then I talk about your attitude to relationships, the way you handle money, what your Sun sign says about your health and, finally, which careers are best for you. Put all that together and you will have a well-rounded picture of yourself.

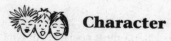 **Character**

If you're a typical Aquarian, you're a law unto yourself. You like to follow your own rules and do your own thing, and if other people don't understand then it's just too bad. This dogmatic approach to life means you can come across as very uncompromising at times, even if you think you're behaving perfectly rationally and everyone else is over-reacting. This is partly because you're ruled by Uranus, the planet of radical views and extremes which encourages you to be true to yourself, no matter whether it makes you unpopular or people think you're odd. You've probably spent all your life knowing that other people don't understand you, so it's nothing new!

You belong to the Air element, making you extremely intelligent and clever. Your natural tendency is to disappear into your thoughts, and you may even retreat into intellectual arguments when you feel at a disadvantage. Talking about ideas, and dealing with the realms of solid facts, can be reassuring for you. You aren't nearly so comfortable when talking about emotions.

You have a strong desire for freedom in all its forms. You want to be free to be whoever you really are, without feeling the need for any window dressing. Although you can be surprisingly resistant to the idea of change at times, nevertheless you can't see any point in sticking to tradition purely for the sake of it. Sometimes you can be years ahead of your time, so you're a lone voice crying in the wilderness. It may take a long time before everyone else agrees with you.

Relationships

Aquarius is one of the most sociable signs of all, especially when it comes to friends. Your sign rules friendship and you really value your chums. You're very choosy about your friends – they must be brainy and interesting to talk to. If all they can talk about is last night's episode of their favourite soap opera, you'll soon move on to someone else.

If you were to write down your idea of what makes a perfect partner, brains would definitely come higher than beauty. Many Aquarians marry or live with someone who was originally a friend. After several years together, your relationship may be based more on solid friendship than fiery passion. That wouldn't suit some signs but it's exactly the way you want it.

One of your greatest qualities is your loyalty. You are steadfast and faithful, and people can always count on you in a crisis. You'll do whatever you can to help out, even if it's only providing a shoulder to cry on. But you expect the same in return and will be upset if you don't get it.

Despite your blunt conversation at times, you can be surprisingly idealistic in relationships. There's nothing cynical about you, and you like to think the best of everyone. You can be shocked and disappointed if they fail to live up to your expectations.

Money

You have a very ambivalent attitude to money. You know that you need it in order to live, but you certainly don't want it for its own sake. The idea of accumulating vast reserves of wealth is abhorrent to you. You are unlikely to want to keep it all for yourself. If you are ever in the happy position of having more money than you know what to do with, you'll want to use it to help others. A strong humanitarian streak flows through you, making you sympathetic to charities and voluntary work.

For a sign that doesn't place a lot of importance on

money, you're surprisingly well organized about it. You keep up to date with what's going on in your bank account and can develop quite an interest in the activities of the stock market.

When looking for things to spend your money on, you can't see the point in false economies. You would rather fork out a fortune on something that's top of the range and will last for years, than spend half that amount on something that isn't very good and will probably eventually conk out. This can cause friction with your partner if they would rather spend the money on other things, such as the groceries.

Health

Most Aquarians are bursting with health. Visiting the doctor is a rare occurrence for you because it's not often that you have anything wrong with you. Even when there is something wrong, you may be more inclined to consult a complementary health practitioner than your GP. However, anything that strikes you as being too wacky or New Age will probably send you into fits of laughter!

Many Aquarians are vegetarians or find some sort of dietary compromise, such as still eating fish and poultry but not eating red meat. Your sign is also very sympathetic to veganism and other dietary regimes, such as food combining. The topic of organic food is likely to make you jump up and down – either with enthusiasm or because you can't see the point of it.

Aquarius rules the circulation and ankles, so these are both areas you need to take care of. If your circulation is sluggish, investigate ways of making it more lively. And if you have weak ankles, look for footwear that will give them some support.

Yoga, Pilates and other exercise techniques are well suited to you, because they enable you to keep supple and healthy in ways that make sense to you. The idea of kicking a ball around a muddy field, for instance, may strike you as bizarre, and you may also wonder why anyone in their right mind would want to go jogging. So it's important for you to find a form of exercise that you enjoy.

Career

Whatever you do for a living, it's essential that it allows you to use your brain. You'll soon become fed up if you're doing something that's mindless or so predictable it makes you want to scream. Ideally, you need a little variety in each day if you're to operate at your best. You also need colleagues who are interesting to talk to – you have no desire to spend time with people whose brains appear to have been replaced with old potato peelings.

Among the careers that would suit you are anything connected with technology and engineering. Many Aquarians have an instinctive understanding of such subjects and thoroughly enjoy playing around with the latest technological equipment. You might be a good electrician, too. New Age techniques and philosophies can appeal to Aquarians. Aquarius is also the sign of astrology, so you might want to take your interest in the subject one step further. Television and radio also have a big attraction for many Aquarians, whichever side of the microphone they happen to be.

Aquarius rules hobbies and pastimes, so you might be able to turn a leisure interest into a full-time job. Alternatively, how about running a business that supplies the equipment for people's hobbies?

LOVE AND THE STARS

Have you ever noticed that you get on better with some signs than others? Perhaps all your friends belong to only a few signs or you've never hit it off with people who come from a particular sign. Or maybe you've recently met someone from a sign that you aren't familiar with at all, and you're wondering how your relationship will develop. Well, this chapter gives you a brief insight into your relationship with the other Sun signs. Check the combination under your own sign's heading first, then read about your relationship from the viewpoint of the other sign to find out what they think of you. It could be very revealing!

At the end of this chapter you'll find two compatibility charts that tell you, at a glance, how well you get on with the other signs as lovers and as friends. Look for the woman's Sun sign along the top of the chart and then find the man's sign down the side. The box where the two meet will show how well they get on together.

Even if your current relationship gets a low score from the charts, that doesn't mean it won't last. It simply indicates that you'll have to work harder at this relationship than at others.

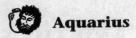 **Aquarius**

Aquarius and **Aquarius** is either wonderful or too much like hard work. One if not both of you must be willing to compromise sometimes, otherwise it will be continual stalemate. You'll have formidable battles of intellect.

Aquarius and **Pisces** is tricky. You don't understand each other, and the more unworldly and unrealistic your Piscean, the more dogmatic and precise you'll become in retaliation. You can easily hurt each other.

Aquarius and **Aries** are great sparring partners and you'll love every minute of it. Your Arien isn't afraid to stand up to you and to fight their corner. They'll also teach you a thing or two about sexual relationships.

Aquarius and **Taurus** is fine all the while you agree with each other. But, at the first hint of dissent, it will be war. Your need for emotional and intellectual freedom will clash with your Taurean's need for closeness.

Aquarius and **Gemini** are firm friends. You enjoy intense intellectual discussions and your Gemini will teach you to be more free-thinking and flexible. Try not to analyse your relationship out of existence.

Aquarius and **Cancer** can be an uneasy combination. You have little in common and don't understand each other. At first you'll enjoy being taken care of by your Cancerian but you may soon feel suffocated and trapped.

Aquarius and **Leo** enjoy each other's company. You love your Leo's exuberance and marvel at their social skills. You'll also be very impressed by their ability to organize you and make your life run so smoothly.

Aquarius and **Virgo** can seem like hard work. It's easier to be friends than lovers because you have such different views of the world. You enjoy pitting your wits against each other in wide-ranging discussions.

Aquarius and **Libra** is great fun and you love sharing ideas. If you get involved in an emotional relationship, your Libran will encourage you to be more demonstrative and less analytical about your feelings.

Aquarius and **Scorpio** is a very powerful combination because you're both so sure of yourselves. In the inevitable disputes, neither of you will want to back down. You may also be turned off by your Scorpio's complicated emotions.

Aquarius and **Sagittarius** enjoy each other's company. You also share a love of learning and both need as much intellectual freedom as you can get. This can be a very enduring relationship, whether it's platonic or passionate.

Aquarius and **Capricorn** will give you lots to think about because you'll be so busy trying to work out what makes each other tick. You may never arrive at an answer! You need to find some middle ground and to compromise.

Pisces

Pisces and **Pisces** is wonderful if you're both prepared to face facts rather than pretend your relationship is something it's not. Your life is likely to be highly romantic and you'll love creating a sophisticated home together.

Pisces and **Aries** will be very trying at times. It may also be painful, since your Arien is unlikely to understand how easily you're hurt. Even so, they will encourage you to grow another layer of skin and to laugh at yourself.

Pisces and **Taurus** is a very sensual combination. You'll bring out the romantic in one another, but there will be times when you'll wish your Taurean were less matter-of-fact, practical and sensible.

Pisces and **Gemini** can have fun together but it's awfully easy for you to feel hurt by your Gemini's glib turns of phrase. You may be happier as friends than lovers because your emotional needs are so different.

Pisces and **Cancer** is super because you both express love in the same way. It's wonderful being with someone who takes such care of you, although your Cancerian may not understand your need to be left alone sometimes.

Pisces and **Leo** find it hard to understand each other. At times you may find your Leo rather grand. You share a pronounced artistic streak and you're both very affectionate, but is that enough to keep you together?

Pisces and **Virgo** can be difficult for you. Your Virgo may trample all over your feelings in their well-meaning efforts to point out your faults and help you to rise above them. It all sounds like a lot of unnecessary criticism to you.

Pisces and **Libra** can be incredibly romantic. You could easily have a heady affair straight out of a Hollywood weepie, but staying together is another matter. You may drift apart because you're reluctant to face up to problems.

Pisces and **Scorpio** is a highly emotional and complex pairing. You're both very deep and sensitive, and it may take a while before you begin to understand each other. Once that happens, you won't look back.

Pisces and **Sagittarius** is dicey because you won't know what to make of your forthright Sagittarian. Why are they so blunt? Can't they see that it upsets you? You may be better as friends who share lots of exploits.

Pisces and **Capricorn** is fine if your Capricorn is happy to show their feelings. But if they're buttoned up or repressed, you won't know how to get through to them. Even so, you'll love the way they provide for you.

Pisces and **Aquarius** may as well be talking different languages for all the sense you make to each other. They enjoy talking about ideas that leave you baffled but will struggle to express their emotions in the way you need.

Aries

Aries and **Aries** is a very energetic combination, and you encourage each other in many different ways. Your relationship is competitive, sexy, exciting and sometimes pretty tempestuous!

Aries and **Taurus** can be difficult because you don't always understand each other. You love your Taurean's loyalty and affection but can feel frustrated if they're a great traditionalist or very stubborn.

Aries and **Gemini** get on like a house on fire and love hatching up new schemes together. But your differing sexual needs could cause problems, especially if your Gemini doesn't share your high sex drive.

Aries and **Cancer** is fine if your Cancerian will give you lots of personal freedom. However, they may be hurt if you aren't at home as much as they'd like, and they'll wonder what you're up to while you're away.

Aries and **Leo** really hit it off well and you'll have a lot of fun together. Sometimes you may wish your Leo would unbend a bit and be less dignified, but you adore the way they love and cherish you. It's great for your ego!

Aries and **Virgo** can be tricky because you have so little in common. You like to rush through life taking each day as it comes while they prefer to plan things in advance and then worry if they're doing the right thing. Irritating!

Aries and **Libra** have a lot to learn from each other. You enjoy the odd skirmish while your Libran prefers to keep the peace. Try to compromise over your differences rather than make them either/or situations.

Aries and **Scorpio** can be very dynamic and sexy together. Power is a huge aphrodisiac for you both so you're greatly attracted to each other. If you're a flirtatious Aries, your Scorpio will soon clip your wings.

Aries and **Sagittarius** are really excited by each other's company. You both adore challenges and will spur one another on to further feats and adventures. Your sex life is lively and interesting, and will keep you pretty busy.

Aries and **Capricorn** may not seem to have much in common on the surface. Yet you are both ambitious and will enjoy watching each other's progress. Sexually, things are surprisingly highly charged and naughty.

Aries and **Aquarius** have a lot of fun together but also share plenty of sparring matches. You get on better as friends than lovers because your Aquarian may not be nearly as interested in sex as you are.

Aries and **Pisces** is one of those tricky combinations that needs a lot of care if it's to succeed. It's horribly easy for you to upset your Piscean, often without realizing it, and you may get bored with having to reassure them so much.

Taurus

Taurus and **Taurus** is great because you're with someone who understands you inside out. Yet although this is comforting at first, it might start to become rather boring after a while, especially if you both like playing it safe.

Taurus and **Gemini** is good for keeping you on your toes, although you may find this tiring in the long term. They need a lot of change and variety, which can unsettle you and make you cling to stability and tradition.

Taurus and **Cancer** is lovely. You both appreciate the same sorts of things in life, such as good food, a loving partner and a cosy home. Once you get together you'll feel as though you've found your true soulmate.

Taurus and **Leo** share a love of luxury and the good things in life. You also know you can trust your Leo to be faithful and loyal, and in return you will shower them with plenty of admiration and moral support.

Taurus and **Virgo** is a very practical combination. Neither of you likes wasting time or money, although you may sometimes wish that your Virgo could be a little less austere and a bit more relaxed. But you still love them.

Taurus and **Libra** can have a very sensual and loving relationship. Neither of you likes conflict and you both need affectionate partners. But you may end up spending a lot of money together on all sorts of luxuries.

Taurus and **Scorpio** is a very powerful combination, especially in the bedroom. You both place a lot of importance on fidelity and loyalty, and you'll both believe that your relationship is the most important thing in your lives.

Taurus and **Sagittarius** don't really understand each other. You enjoy your home comforts and are generally content with life, while your Sagittarian always finds the grass is greener on the other side of the fence.

Taurus and **Capricorn** have a lot in common. You're both lusty, earthy and full of common sense. If you aren't careful, your relationship could get bogged down in practicalities, making you neglect the fun side of things.

Taurus and **Aquarius** struggle to appreciate each other. You enjoy sticking to the status quo whenever possible, while your Aquarian is always thinking of the future. You're both very stubborn, so rows can end in stalemate.

Taurus and **Pisces** is fine if your Piscean has their feet on the ground, because then you'll enjoy their sensitivity. But if they're very vague or other-worldly, you'll soon get annoyed and lose patience with them.

Taurus and **Aries** isn't the easiest combination for you. Although you enjoy your Arien's enthusiasm, it can wear a bit thin sometimes, especially when they're keen on something that you think is unrealistic or too costly.

Gemini

Gemini and **Gemini** can be great fun or one big headache. You both crave variety and busy lives, but if you're both very sociable you may rarely see each other. Your sex life may also fizzle out over time.

Gemini and **Cancer** is tricky if you're lovers rather than friends. Although you'll adore your Cancerian's displays of affection at first, after a while they may seem rather clingy or will make you feel trapped.

Gemini and **Leo** have lots of fun together. You genuinely like and love one another, although you may secretly be amused sometimes by your Leo's regal behaviour and want to give them some gentle teasing.

Gemini and **Virgo** hit it off surprisingly well. There's so much for you to talk about and plenty of scope for having a good laugh. You're tremendous friends, whether your relationship is sexual or purely platonic.

Gemini and **Libra** is one of the most enjoyable combinations of all for you. You can encourage your easy-going Libran to be more assertive while they help you to relax, and also bring out the romance in your soul.

Gemini and **Scorpio** make uncomfortable bedfellows but good friends. You have very little in common sexually but are intrigued by each other's minds. You share an insatiable curiosity about human nature.

Gemini and **Sagittarius** have a really good time together. You especially enjoy learning new things from one another and never run out of things to talk about. Travel and books are just two of your many shared enthusiasms.

Gemini and **Capricorn** isn't very easy because you're so different. At first you're intrigued by your Capricorn's responsibility and common sense, but after a while they may seem a little staid or stuffy for you.

Gemini and **Aquarius** are fantastic friends. You're used to having the upper hand intellectually with people but here is someone who makes you think and encourages you to look at life in a new way.

Gemini and **Pisces** can be tricky because it's easy to hurt your Piscean's feelings without even realizing it. Neither of you is very keen on facing up to harsh reality, which causes problems if you both avoid dealing with the facts.

Gemini and **Aries** is tremendous fun and you'll spend a lot of time laughing. If even half the plans you make come to fruition, you'll have a fantastic time together with never a dull moment.

Gemini and **Taurus** can make you wonder what you're doing wrong. Your Taurean may seem bemused or even slightly alarmed by you, and positively threatened by your need for as much variety in your life as possible.

 **Cancer**

Cancer and **Cancer** is wonderful because you're able to take refuge in each other. You'll lavish a lot of time and effort on your home. Problems will arise if one of you doesn't get on well with the other one's family or friends.

Cancer and **Leo** share a love of family life, and you may even agree to give it priority over everything else. You'll be very proud of your Leo's achievements but will fret if these take them away from home too often.

Cancer and **Virgo** have a lot to teach each other. You'll learn from your Virgo how to do things methodically and carefully, and you'll encourage them to be more demonstrative and loving. It should work well!

Cancer and **Libra** is great if you have shared goals. You both understand the importance of ambition and will readily support one another. You enjoy being with someone who isn't afraid to show their affections.

Cancer and **Scorpio** is a very emotional and satisfying pairing. You know you can reveal your true feelings to your Scorpio, and you'll encourage them to do the same with you. Sexually, you'll really be in your element.

Cancer and **Sagittarius** find it hard to appreciate each other. You may even feel as though you come from different planets because you operate on a very emotional level while your Sagittarian prefers to stick to the facts.

Cancer and **Capricorn** is a case of opposites attracting. You both need what the other one can offer, and you'll be especially pleased if your Capricorn's capacity for hard work will provide a roof over your head and a stable home.

Cancer and **Aquarius** can be quirky friends but you'll struggle to sustain an emotional relationship because you're chalk and cheese. Your need for love and reassurance may be very difficult for your Aquarian to deal with.

Cancer and **Pisces** are really happy together. It's great knowing that you're with someone who understands your deep emotional needs and your complicated personality. You'll also revel in taking care of your Piscean.

Cancer and **Aries** can work if you both make allowances for each other. You need to give your Aries a lot of freedom because they'll get very angry if they feel they're tied to your apron strings.

Cancer and **Taurus** is a marriage made in heaven. You both need a happy, comfortable home and you also share a love of food. Your relationship may be so self-sufficient that you barely need anyone else in your lives.

Cancer and **Gemini** is OK if you don't spend too much time together! You'll feel slightly threatened by your Gemini's need for an active and independent social life, and they'll resent being expected to spend so much time at home.

Leo

Leo and **Leo** is a very strong combination but there could be a few battles for power every now and then. After all, neither of you likes to relinquish the reins and hand over control to anyone else. Even so, you'll have a lot of fun.

Leo and **Virgo** is fine if you're prepared for some give and take but it won't be very easy if each of you stands your ground. You'll be pleased if your Virgo tries to help or advise you, but will be hurt if this turns to undue criticism.

Leo and **Libra** is a delicious pairing because it brings together the two signs of love. You'll adore being with someone who is so considerate, although their lack of decisiveness may sometimes make you grit your teeth with irritation.

Leo and **Scorpio** is wonderful until you have a row. At that point, you'll both refuse to budge an inch and admit that you might be in the wrong. You both set a lot of store by status symbols, which could work out expensive.

Leo and **Sagittarius** is great for keeping each other amused. You're both enthusiastic, intuitive and expansive, although you could sometimes be annoyed if your Sagittarian's social life prevents you seeing much of them.

Leo and **Capricorn** share a tremendous love of family and you'll enjoy creating a happy home together. Don't expect your Capricorn to be instinctively demonstrative: you may have to teach them to be more open.

Leo and **Aquarius** understand each other even if you don't always see eye to eye. Sometimes you can be left speechless by your plain-speaking Aquarian, and disappointed by their occasional reluctance to be cuddly.

Leo and **Pisces** bring out each other's creativity. This is a superb artistic partnership but may not be such good news if you're trying to maintain a sexual relationship because you have so little in common.

Leo and **Aries** have terrific fun together and will share many adventures. You'll enjoy making lots of plans, even if they don't always work out. You'll also spend plenty of money on lavishly entertaining your friends.

Leo and **Taurus** is the sort of relationship that makes you feel you know where you stand. You love knowing that your Taurean is steadfast and true, and that together you make a formidable team.

Leo and **Gemini** is a fun-filled combination that you really enjoy. You're stunned by your Gemini's endless inventiveness and their versatility, although you may secretly believe that they spread themselves too thin.

Leo and **Cancer** is great if you both need a comfortable and cosy home. But you may soon feel hemmed in if your Cancerian wants to restrict your social circle to nothing but family and close friends. You need more scope than that.

 **Virgo**

Virgo and **Virgo** can endure many storms together, even though it's tough going at times. Here is someone who completely understands your interesting mixture of quirky individualism and the need to conform.

Virgo and **Libra** get on well together up to a point but can then come unstuck. It annoys you when your Libran fails to stand up for themselves and you don't understand why they're so touchy when you point out their faults.

Virgo and **Scorpio** are both fascinated by the details of life and you'll spend many happy hours analysing people's characters. Try not to be too brusque when pointing out some of your Scorpio's stranger points; they won't like it!

Virgo and **Sagittarius** is a very sociable pairing and you'll enjoy being together. You'll also have some fascinating conversations in which you both learn a lot. Sexually, it will either be great or ghastly.

Virgo and **Capricorn** really understand each other. You appreciate your Capricorn's reliability but worry about their workaholic tendencies. You'll both benefit from being openly affectionate and loving with one another.

Virgo and **Aquarius** enjoy discussing just about everything under the sun. But you'll quickly get irritated by your Aquarian's idiosyncratic views and their insistence that they're always right. Surely if anyone's right, you are?

Virgo and **Pisces** is not the easiest combination you can choose. If your Piscean finds it hard to face up to reality, you won't be sympathetic because you simply can't understand such an ostrich-like attitude.

Virgo and **Aries** struggle to get on well as close partners. You simply don't understand each other. They make a mess and you like things to be tidy. They rush into things and you like to take your time. There is little common ground.

Virgo and **Taurus** love each other's company. You both like to keep your feet on the ground and you share a healthy respect for money. You also have a very raunchy time in the bedroom although you don't advertise that fact.

Virgo and **Gemini** is a super combination for friendship or business. You think along similar lines and both excel at being flexible. However, in a sexual relationship you may fail to appreciate each other's finer points.

Virgo and **Cancer** is a great team. You like to take care of worldly matters while your Cancerian creates a happy and cosy home. If they collect a lot of clutter you'll think of it as dust traps rather than delightful keepsakes.

Virgo and **Leo** find it hard to understand each other because you're so different. You may secretly find your Leo rather ostentatious and there could be rows about the amount of money they spend. Try to live and let live.

 Libra

Libra and **Libra** get on really well provided at least one of you is decisive and able to say what they think sometimes. You'll appreciate one another's consideration, sensitivity and intelligence. A great combination!

Libra and **Scorpio** are good friends but may not understand each other's sexual and emotional needs. You may feel uncomfortable with the brooding, intense moods of your Scorpio, wishing they took things less seriously.

Libra and **Sagittarius** have lots of fun together, especially when it comes to discussing ideas and taking off on jaunts. However, you could be rather nonplussed, and possibly even hurt, by your Sagittarian's blunt comments.

Libra and **Capricorn** get on famously if you share goals. You understand each other's need to work hard towards your ambitions. But you'll have to coax your Capricorn into being as demonstrative and loving as you'd like.

Libra and **Aquarius** appreciate one another's minds. You may be better friends than lovers, because you could be bemused and hurt if your Aquarian is unnerved by your need for romance and idealism.

Libra and **Pisces** share a need for peace and harmony. You'll adore being with someone who's so artistic and sensitive, but you both need to balance your romantic natures with hefty doses of reality every now and then.

Libra and **Aries** are a great example of how opposites can attract. You admire the way your brave Arien can be so outspoken, and they may even manage to teach you to stand up for yourself.

Libra and **Taurus** share a love of beauty and an appreciation of the finer things in life. At first you may think you've found your perfect partner, although you may get irritated if your Taurean is very placid.

Libra and **Gemini** get on well in every sort of relationship. You're amused by your Gemini's butterfly ability to flit from one topic to the next and will enjoy encouraging them to discover the romance that lurks inside them.

Libra and **Cancer** enjoy one another's company. You love the way your Cancerian so obviously cares about your welfare and happiness, and it does you good to be the one who's fussed over for a change.

Libra and **Leo** can be a very expensive combination! Neither of you is frightened to spend money and together you can have a field day. Emotionally, you revel in one another's company because you're both born romantics.

Libra and **Virgo** have to make a lot of effort to appreciate one another. You can understand the importance of attending to details but you may secretly think that your Virgo sometimes is too much of a nit-picker.

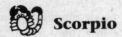 **Scorpio**

Scorpio and **Scorpio** feel safe with each other. You both know what you're capable of, good and bad. It's great to be with someone who matches you for intensity, but you might wind each other up and feed each other's neuroses.

Scorpio and **Sagittarius** can miss each other by miles. Even as friends, it's hard to understand one another. You like to zero in on the details while your Sagittarian prefers to take a broad view of the entire situation.

Scorpio and **Capricorn** bring out the best in one another, but it can take a little time. You enjoy the serious side to your Capricorn but you can also have some great laughs together. You also love knowing that they're so reliable.

Scorpio and **Aquarius** can have some terrific rows! You both have a tendency to be dogmatic and it's even worse when you get together. You can feel threatened if your Aquarian isn't as openly affectionate as you'd like.

Scorpio and **Pisces** share some powerful moments together. You love the complexity and sensitivity of your Piscean but will soon become suspicious if you think they're holding out on you or are playing games behind your back.

Scorpio and **Aries** is a tempestuous combination. Your temper builds up from a slow burn while your Arien will have a quick tantrum and then forget about it. Sexually, you'll have more than met your match.

Scorpio and **Taurus** complement each other in many ways. You're both loyal and loving, and you both need a secure home. However, problems will arise if one or both of you is possessive and jealous.

Scorpio and **Gemini** hit it off as friends but will struggle to stick together as lovers. You like to explore the nitty-gritty of situations while your Gemini apparently prefers to skim the surface. You may wonder if you can trust them.

Scorpio and **Cancer** can enjoy a highly emotional and satisfying relationship. You understand one another's needs and will take great delight in creating a stable and happy home life together.

Scorpio and **Leo** is tricky if you both want to rule the roost. Neither of you likes to relinquish control of situations, which can lead to some stormy battles for power. At times you may be jealous of your Leo's huge circle of friends.

Scorpio and **Virgo** have some wonderfully analytical conversations. You both enjoy digging below the surface to find out what's really going on. If it's a sexual relationship, its success will rest on what happens in the bedroom.

Scorpio and **Libra** appreciate one another but you may sometimes wish your Libran could be more forceful and dynamic. It will drive you mad when they sit on the fence or bend over backwards to please everyone.

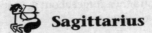 **Sagittarius**

Sagittarius and **Sagittarius** will either have a whale of a time or never see each other. If you both have wide-ranging interests, it may be difficult to make enough time for one another and you may eventually drift apart.

Sagittarius and **Capricorn** think of each other as a creature from another planet. You like your Capricorn's common sense but will soon get fed up if they cling to tradition, are a workaholic or never want to take any risks.

Sagittarius and **Aquarius** have a fantastic time together. You share so many interests that there is always something to talk about, with some far-ranging discussions. But you may wish your Aquarian were less pedantic.

Sagittarius and **Pisces** enjoy being friends but it can be difficult to understand each other as lovers. You like your Piscean's sensitivity but wish they weren't quite so easily hurt when you make off-the-cuff comments.

Sagittarius and **Aries** is great fun. You'll have all sorts of adventures together, with exotic holidays a particular indulgence. You're both pretty outspoken and your no-holds-barred rows will raise the roof.

Sagittarius and **Taurus** struggle to hit it off. You're so different that it's hard to find much common ground. If your Taurean is possessive, you'll soon feel trapped and want to break free, or decide to do things behind their back.

Sagittarius and **Gemini** is a super combination. You have masses in common and are endlessly intrigued by one another. However, you must be friends as well as lovers, otherwise you may soon get bored with each other.

Sagittarius and **Cancer** can't make each other out at all. You're mystified by your Cancerian's constant need for their home and family, and will be irritated if you think they're too parochial and unadventurous.

Sagittarius and **Leo** revel in each other's company, especially when it comes to having fun. This can be an expensive pairing because you both enjoy living it up whenever you get the chance. Shopping trips will also be costly.

Sagittarius and **Virgo** is OK up to a point. You enjoy each other's brains but you'll soon lose patience if your Virgo is very finicky and anxious. You like to let your hair down but they may always worry about the consequences.

Sagittarius and **Libra** like each other, whether as friends, family or lovers. You have enough similarities to find some common ground but enough differences to keep things interesting. It's an intriguing combination.

Sagittarius and **Scorpio** try and fail to understand each other. You like to take life as it comes and can't stand your Scorpio's tendency to plot things in advance. You'll hate it if they're suspicious or jealous of you.

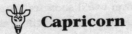 **Capricorn**

Capricorn and **Capricorn** feel very safe together. At last you're with someone who understands you, and who's as reliable and responsible as you. However, this may mean that your work clashes with your relationship.

Capricorn and **Aquarius** is either a big hit or a big no-no. You both need to compromise and to be willing to learn from each other for it to work. Your love of convention will be sorely challenged by your radical Aquarian.

Capricorn and **Pisces** can learn a lot from each other as friends. You'll learn to be more sensitive and open-minded. However, you'll soon be turned off if your Piscean is reluctant to face up to facts and be realistic.

Capricorn and **Aries** support each other in many ways. You're both ambitious and will respect one another's goals. You'll enjoy teaching your Arien to be more responsible, and they'll teach you how to play.

Capricorn and **Taurus** feel safe with one another. You both understand the importance of tradition and share the need to do things properly. You can get surprisingly earthy and intense in the bedroom.

Capricorn and **Gemini** don't really hit it off. You're amused by your Gemini but you may secretly think they're too flighty and superficial for you. It's difficult to find much common ground sexually or emotionally.

Capricorn and **Cancer** really enjoy each other's company. You both adore having someone to take care of, and if anyone can dissuade you from working round the clock it's a home-cooking, sensuous and affectionate Cancerian.

Capricorn and **Leo** both like the best in life but you won't be as willing to pay for it as your Leo. In fact, you may be seriously worried by their extravagance and also slightly wearied by their demanding social life.

Capricorn and **Virgo** go together like bread and butter. However, there may not be much jam if you're both careful with your money. If you share a home you'll want it to be traditional, with conventional family values.

Capricorn and **Libra** have a healthy respect for each other. You love your Libran's diplomacy and tact, because you know you can take them anywhere and they'll fit in. They'll also encourage you to open up emotionally.

Capricorn and **Scorpio** is a very businesslike pairing. You excel at making money together, no matter what your relationship. Sometimes you can be put off by the intense and complex passions of your Scorpio.

Capricorn and **Sagittarius** can be strange. You like each other for your curiosity value if not much else. Even so, your Sagittarian will teach you to be more broad-minded and relaxed, if you let them.

Compatibility in Love and Sex at a glance

F M	♈	♉	♊	♋	♌	♍	♎	♏	♐	♑	♒	♓
♈	8	5	9	7	9	4	7	8	9	7	7	3
♉	6	8	4	10	7	8	8	7	3	8	2	8
♊	8	2	7	3	8	7	9	4	9	4	9	4
♋	5	10	4	8	6	5	6	8	2	9	2	8
♌	9	8	9	7	7	4	9	6	8	7	9	6
♍	4	8	6	4	4	7	6	7	7	9	4	4
♎	7	8	10	7	8	5	9	6	9	6	10	6
♏	7	9	4	7	6	6	7	10	5	6	5	7
♐	9	4	10	4	9	7	8	4	9	6	9	5
♑	7	8	4	9	6	8	6	4	4	8	4	5
♒	8	6	9	4	9	4	9	6	8	7	8	2
♓	7	6	7	9	6	7	6	9	7	5	4	9

1 = the pits
10 = the peaks

Key

♈ – Aries
♉ – Taurus
♊ – Gemini
♋ – Cancer
♌ – Leo
♍ – Virgo

♎ – Libra
♏ – Scorpio
♐ – Sagittarius
♑ – Capricorn
♒ – Aquarius
♓ – Pisces

Compatibility in Friendship at a glance

F M	♈	♉	♊	♋	♌	♍	♎	♏	♐	♑	♒	♓
♈	8	5	10	5	9	3	7	8	9	6	8	5
♉	6	9	6	10	7	8	7	6	4	9	3	9
♊	9	3	9	4	9	8	10	5	10	5	10	6
♋	6	9	4	9	5	4	6	9	4	10	3	9
♌	10	7	9	6	9	4	8	6	9	6	9	7
♍	5	9	8	4	4	8	5	8	8	10	5	6
♎	8	9	10	8	8	6	9	5	9	6	10	7
♏	7	8	5	8	7	7	6	9	4	5	6	8
♐	9	5	10	4	10	8	8	4	10	7	9	6
♑	6	9	5	10	6	9	5	5	4	9	5	6
♒	9	6	10	5	9	5	9	7	9	5	9	3
♓	6	7	6	10	6	8	7	9	8	6	4	10

1 = the pits
10 = the peaks

Key

♈ – Aries
♉ – Taurus
♊ – Gemini
♋ – Cancer
♌ – Leo
♍ – Virgo

♎ – Libra
♏ – Scorpio
♐ – Sagittarius
♑ – Capricorn
♒ – Aquarius
♓ – Pisces

FAMILY AND FRIENDS

What does your Sun sign say about your relationship with your family and friends? Do you value family far above friends, or do you have the sort of family that makes you glad you can choose your friends? Read on to discover how you relate to those important people in your life.

Aquarius

Friendship is one of your greatest gifts. You excel at making friends and you attract people from all walks of life and all ages. You can see nothing odd about a forty-year age gap between friends, nor are you interested in choosing influential or wealthy friends because of what they might be able to give you. If you like someone, you like them, and that's all there is to it. This can sometimes cause problems if your partner doesn't understand or is jealous because they consider your best friend to be competition for their affections. As far as family are concerned, you enjoy seeing them every now and then but aren't overly family-minded. You make a point of keeping in regular contact with the relatives you like but aren't too worried if you can't see much of the others.

 **Pisces**

You enjoy developing strong family ties because you like the sense of continuity it gives you. It's great to be with people who you've known for most, if not all, of your life. You would be very fortunate if all your relatives were lovable and likeable, but you do your best to tolerate the ones who you aren't so keen on. You lavish a lot of love on the ones who are your favourites, and will find ways to let them know that you think they're special. Yet you're so sensitive to the plight of lame ducks that you'll feel sorry for the people you don't like, probably because you realize they aren't very popular with anyone. You choose your friends carefully, preferring people who are on your emotional wavelength and who share your view of the world.

 Aries

Being born under the sign of Aries makes you affectionate, enthusiastic and impulsive, and you bring all these qualities into your relationships with family and friends. You adore children and make a special effort to get on well with them. You're perfectly happy romping around on the floor with them or taking them on long walks and teaching them about nature. You're always prepared to think the best of people and you're ready to give them the benefit of the doubt if there are any questions about their behaviour. You are essentially trusting, which means you can be badly hurt when people betray that trust. Yet you don't seem to learn from your mistakes and you're quite likely to do the same things all over again, telling yourself that this time it will be different. When it isn't, you're very disappointed.

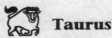

Taurus

Your family mean the world to you and you'll do whatever you can to support them. Part of this support means providing for their daily needs, so you're perfectly prepared to work round the clock if that's what it takes to feed and clothe them. You are also extremely loyal and steadfast, so loved ones know they can count on you to be there when they need you. In return, you need to be loved and appreciated. Sometimes, an element of possessiveness may creep into the equation, making you treat your loved ones as though they're your personal belongings. For instance, you may secretly feel as though you've been supplanted when your children are old enough to fall in love, or you might be rather worried if your friends don't spend as much time with you as you'd like. If you relax, you'll realize that there's more than enough love to go round.

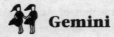

Gemini

As one of the most sociable signs in the zodiac, you have an instinctive need for kindred spirits in your life. You need people to bounce ideas off and to chat to, and you won't really care if they're friends or family if you like them. For instance, you may be best friends with your cousin, knowing that you would have liked him or her even if you weren't related. You enjoy keeping up with the latest gossip about all the people in your life, so family occasions can be great fun for you because you're able to find out what's going on. Children are strongly attracted to you because they sense your own childlike nature, and you'll happily spend hours playing with them or reading to them. When you're away from family and friends, you'll do your best to keep in touch with them by phone, letter or e-mail.

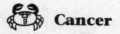 **Cancer**

If you're a typical Cancerian, your friends and family mean the world to you. You may not even have many friends; you may spend so much time with your family that you don't feel the need for anyone else in your life. In turn, you may be slightly offended when members of the family have outside interests because you think they shouldn't need them. Blood is definitely thicker than water, as far as you're concerned. If you don't get on well with your relatives or you're separated from them for some reason, you'll create your own family group from friends and colleagues. You're very warm and caring, and are always concerned about other people's welfare. Sometimes this can seem rather claustrophobic to others, even though you're doing it from the best of motives. So try to avoid smother love!

 Leo

You're very family-minded and you love surrounding yourself with all your nearest and dearest. You adore being with children and will pay a lot of attention to their upbringing, encouraging them to express themselves and be creative. Yet you are also a stickler for good manners so will teach them to behave properly and not let you down. You're strict when you think the occasion demands it but try to be as loving and affectionate as possible. Friends are another essential part of your life and you enjoy making a big fuss of them. You place a lot of importance on loyalty and trust, and will be bitterly hurt if a loved one betrays you or is harshly critical of you. You may forgive them once or twice, but it will be a different story if they continue to do it.

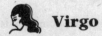 **Virgo**

It may not always be easy for you to show your feelings but that doesn't mean you don't have them. You can be very loving and affectionate, but you often aren't very demonstrative. In fact, you can feel quite uncomfortable when you're with people who are very lovey-dovey because it just isn't your style. You're very discriminating, even with close members of the family, so you may find that you love them but don't really like them very much. If you aren't keen on a relative, you'll be polite but will try to restrict the amount of time you spend with them. When it comes to friends, you choose them wisely and well. You won't squander your affections and are unlikely to be chums with anyone who's boring, lousy company or a complete numbskull.

Libra

Harmonious relationships are essential to your well-being, no matter who they're with. It's important to you that you get on as well with your family as your friends, and you'll feel quite churned up when you have a disagreement with anyone. You don't enjoy spending a lot of time on your own, so you'll like it if your family can give you plenty of company. You'll do your best to instil courtesy and good manners in your children. When choosing your friends, you're attracted to people who are bright, witty and great company. It's very easy for you to make friends because you're naturally so charming and outgoing. The difficulty for you may be in managing to keep up with all your chums because you've got so many of them.

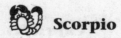 **Scorpio**

As with every other area of your life, you take your relationships with your friends and family very seriously. You may not be enamoured with all your family but you will treat them with respect and consideration, hoping that they'll never guess your real feelings about them. Yet you'll be ultra-loyal to the members of your family who you really care about, and they'll know that they can rely on you completely when the chips are down. When you have children, you dote on them but you're very strict with them too. As for friends, you tend to make them for life. You may still be in touch with friends you made when you were very young. However, if someone betrays you or seriously displeases you, you will sever all connection with them if needs be and never give them another chance.

Sagittarius

You're so outgoing and gregarious that you can't imagine not having lots of friends. They probably come from many different walks of life and cultures because you aren't interested in race, religion, sexuality or any of the other social divisions that tend to separate people. However, you won't spend much time with anyone who is narrow-minded or deeply negative, and they also won't be a boon companion if they've got fluff for brains. When it comes to your relatives, you like seeing them but they aren't the be-all and end-all of your existence. It's a different story if you have children, because you'll lavish tremendous amounts of love and energy on them, and will adore teaching them all about the world. If you can transmit some of your optimism and enthusiasm to them, you'll be very pleased with yourself.

 Capricorn

Blood ties mean a lot to you and it will be a source of great sadness if you aren't as close to your family as you would like. Even so, you will do your best to keep in touch with everyone because, deep down, you believe that stable families are the bedrock of society. When bringing up your own family you will do your best to teach your children to respect their elders, and will be happiest with a traditional family unit. If you are separated from your family, you will establish a strong network of friends who feel like family or the next best thing. You're a very faithful, loving and dependable friend, although you're a lot more sensitive than people may think. You don't wear your heart on your sleeve but you're still easily hurt.

BORN ON THE CUSP?

Were you born on the cusp of Aquarius – at the beginning or end of the sign? If so, you may have spent years wondering which sign you belong to. Are you an Aquarian, a Capricorn or a Piscean? Different horoscope books and columns can give different dates for when the Sun moves into each sign, leaving you utterly confused. Yet none of these dates is wrong, as you'll discover in a minute. Checking your birth date, and time if you know it, in the list given in this chapter will allow you to solve the mystery at long last!

Many people believe that the Sun moves like clockwork from one sign to another on a specific day each year. But this isn't always true. For instance, let's look at the dates for the sign of Aquarius. On the cover of this book I give them as 21 January to 18 February. Very often, the Sun will obediently change signs on these days but sometimes it won't. It can move from Capricorn into Aquarius on 20 or 21 January and it can move into Pisces on 18 or 19 February.

So how can you find out which sign you belong to if you were born on the cusp of Aquarius? The only information you need is the place, year, day and the time of your birth if you know it. It helps to have the time of birth because if the Sun did move signs on your birthday, you can see whether it moved before or after you were born. If you don't have an exact time, even knowing whether it was morning or afternoon can be a help. For instance, if you were born in the morning and the Sun didn't move signs on your birthday until the afternoon, that will be enough information to tell you which sign is yours.

You need to know the place in case you were born outside the United Kingdom and have to convert its local time zone to British time. This information is easily available in many diaries and reference books.

Four Simple Steps to Find your Sun Sign

1 Write down the year, day, time and place of your birth, in that order.
2 If you were born outside the United Kingdom, you must convert your birth date and time to British time by adding or subtracting the relevant number of hours from your birth time to convert it to British time. This may take your birthday into the following day or back to the previous day. If so, write down this new date and time because that will be the one you use in the following calculations. If summer time was operating you must deduct the relevant number of hours to convert your birth time to Greenwich Mean Time (GMT).
3 If you were born in Britain, look up your year of birth in the list of British Summer Time (BST) changes to see if BST was operating when you were born. If it was, subtract the appropriate number of hours from your birth time to convert it to GMT. This may give you a different time and/or date of birth.
4 Look up your year of birth in the Annual Sun Sign Changes list. If you were born within these dates and times, you are an Aquarian. If you were born outside them, you are either a Capricorn if you were born in January, or a Piscean if you were born in February.

Two Examples

Here are a couple of examples so you can see how the process works. Let's say we're looking for the Sun sign of Bill, who was born in the UK on 21 January 1970 at 00:45. Start by checking the list of British Summer Time (BST) dates to see if BST was operating at the time of his birth. It was, so you have to subtract one hour from his birth time to convert it to GMT. This gives him a birth time of 23:45 on the previous day – therefore, his GMT birthday is 20 January and his GMT birth time is 23:45. Write this down, so you don't forget it. Now turn to the Annual Sun Sign Changes list and look for 1970, his year of birth. In that year, the Sun moved into Aquarius on 20 January at 11:24, and Bill's GMT birth time was at 23:45 that evening, so he is an Aquarian. However, if he had been born on 20 January 1970 at 03:30 (which gives him a GMT birth time of 02:30), the Sun would have been in Capricorn so he would be a Capricorn.

But what would his sign be if he were born on 19 February 1960 at 15:30? (Note the change of year.) First, check the dates in the BST list for 1960 to see if it was operating at the time of his birth. It wasn't, so his birth time and day remain the same. Now look up the Sun sign dates for 1960. Look at the February date. The Sun was in Aquarius until 19 February at 15:26. So Bill was born just after the Sun had moved into Pisces, making him a Piscean.

Dates for British Summer Time

If your birthday falls within these dates and times, you were born during BST and will have to convert your birth time back to GMT. To do this, subtract one hour from your birth time. If you were born during a period that is marked *, you must subtract two hours from your birth time to convert it to GMT. All times are given in BST, using the 24-hour clock.

1920 28 Mar, 02:00–25 Oct, 01:59 inc	**1952** 20 Apr, 02:00–26 Oct, 01:59 inc
1921 3 Apr, 02:00–3 Oct, 01:59 inc	**1953** 19 Apr, 02:00–4 Oct, 01:59 inc
1922 26 Mar, 02:00–8 Oct, 01:59 inc	**1954** 11 Apr, 02:00–3 Oct, 01:59 inc
1923 22 Apr, 02:00–16 Sep, 01:59 inc	**1955** 17 Apr, 02:00–2 Oct, 01:59 inc
1924 13 Apr, 02:00–21 Sep, 01:59 inc	**1956** 22 Apr, 02:00–7 Oct, 01:59 inc
1925 19 Apr, 02:00–4 Oct, 01:59 inc	**1957** 14 Apr, 02:00–6 Oct, 01:59 inc
1926 18 Apr, 02:00–3 Oct, 01:59 inc	**1958** 20 Apr, 02:00–5 Oct, 01:59 inc
1927 10 Apr, 02:00–2 Oct, 01:59 inc	**1959** 19 Apr, 02:00–4 Oct, 01:59 inc
1928 22 Apr, 02:00–7 Oct, 01:59 inc	**1960** 10 Apr, 02:00–2 Oct, 01:59 inc
1929 21 Apr, 02:00–6 Oct, 01:59 inc	**1961** 26 Mar, 02:00–29 Oct, 01:59 inc
1930 13 Apr, 02:00–5 Oct, 01:59 inc	**1962** 25 Mar, 02:00–28 Oct, 01:59 inc
1931 19 Apr, 02:00–4 Oct, 01:59 inc	**1963** 31 Mar, 02:00–27 Oct, 01:59 inc
1932 17 Apr, 02:00–2 Oct, 01:59 inc	**1964** 22 Mar, 02:00–25 Oct, 01:59 inc
1933 9 Apr, 02:00–8 Oct, 01:59 inc	**1965** 21 Mar, 02:00–24 Oct, 01:59 inc
1934 22 Apr, 02:00–7 Oct, 01:59 inc	**1966** 20 Mar, 02:00–23 Oct, 01:59 inc
1935 14 Apr, 02:00–6 Oct, 01:59 inc	**1967** 19 Mar, 02:00–29 Oct, 01:59 inc
1936 19 Apr, 02:00–4 Oct, 01:59 inc	**1968** 18 Feb, 02:00–31 Dec, 23:59 inc
1937 18 Apr, 02:00–3 Oct, 01:59 inc	**1969** 1 Jan, 00:00–31 Dec, 23:59 inc
1938 10 Apr, 02:00–2 Oct, 01:59 inc	**1970** 1 Jan, 00:00–31 Dec, 23:59 inc
1939 16 Apr, 02:00–19 Nov, 01:59 inc	**1971** 1 Jan, 00:00–31 Oct, 01:59 inc
1940 25 Feb, 02:00–31 Dec, 23:59 inc	**1972** 19 Mar, 02:00–29 Oct, 01:59 inc
1941 1 Jan, 00:00–4 May, 01:59 inc	**1973** 18 Mar, 02:00–28 Oct, 01:59 inc
1941 4 May, 02:00–10 Aug, 01:59 inc*	**1974** 17 Mar, 02:00–27 Oct, 01:59 inc
1941 10 Aug, 02:00–31 Dec, 23:59 inc	**1975** 16 Mar, 02:00–26 Oct, 01:59 inc
1942 1 Jan, 00:00–5 Apr, 01:59 inc	**1976** 21 Mar, 02:00–24 Oct, 01:59 inc
1942 5 Apr, 02:00–9 Aug, 01:59 inc*	**1977** 20 Mar, 02:00–23 Oct, 01:59 inc
1942 9 Aug, 02:00–31 Dec, 23:59 inc	**1978** 19 Mar, 02:00–29 Oct, 01:59 inc
1943 1 Jan, 00:00–4 Apr, 01:59 inc	**1979** 18 Mar, 02:00–28 Oct, 01:59 inc
1943 4 Apr, 02:00–15 Aug, 01:59 inc*	**1980** 16 Mar, 02:00–26 Oct, 01:59 inc
1943 15 Aug, 02:00–31 Dec, 23:59 inc	**1981** 29 Mar, 01:00–25 Oct, 00:59 inc
1944 1 Jan, 00:00–2 Apr, 01:59 inc	**1982** 28 Mar, 01:00–24 Oct, 00:59 inc
1944 2 Apr, 02:00–17 Sep, 01:59 inc*	**1983** 27 Mar, 01:00–23 Oct, 00:59 inc
1944 17 Sep, 02:00–31 Dec, 23:59 inc	**1984** 25 Mar, 01:00–28 Oct, 00:59 inc
1945 1 Jan, 02:00–2 Apr, 01:59 inc	**1985** 31 Mar, 01:00–27 Oct, 00:59 inc
1945 2 Apr, 02:00–15 Jul, 01:59 inc*	**1986** 30 Mar, 01:00–26 Oct, 00:59 inc
1945 15 Jul, 02:00–7 Oct, 01:59 inc	**1987** 29 Mar, 01:00–25 Oct, 00:59 inc
1946 14 Apr, 02:00–6 Oct, 01:59 inc	**1988** 27 Mar, 01:00–23 Oct, 00:59 inc
1947 16 Mar, 02:00–13 Apr, 01:59 inc	**1989** 26 Mar, 01:00–29 Oct, 00:59 inc
1947 13 Apr, 02:00–10 Aug, 01:59 inc*	**1990** 25 Mar, 01:00–28 Oct, 00:59 inc
1947 10 Aug, 02:00–2 Nov, 01:59 inc	**1991** 31 Mar, 01:00–27 Oct, 00:59 inc
1948 14 Mar, 02:00–31 Oct, 01:59 inc	**1992** 29 Mar, 01:00–25 Oct, 00:59 inc
1949 3 Apr, 02:00–30 Oct, 01:59 inc	**1993** 28 Mar, 01:00–24 Oct, 00:59 inc
1950 16 Apr, 02:00–22 Oct, 01:59 inc	**1994** 27 Mar, 01:00–23 Oct, 00:59 inc
1951 15 Apr, 02:00–21 Oct, 01:59 inc	**1995** 26 Mar, 01:00–22 Oct, 00:59 inc

1996 31 Mar, 01:00–27 Oct, 00:59 inc　**2000** 26 Mar, 01:00–29 Oct, 00:59 inc
1997 30 Mar, 01:00–26 Oct, 00:59 inc　**2001** 25 Mar, 01:00–28 Oct, 00:59 inc
1998 29 Mar, 01:00–25 Oct, 00:59 inc　**2002** 31 Mar, 01:00–27 Oct, 00:59 inc
1999 28 Mar, 01:00–31 Oct, 00:59 inc　**2003** 30 Mar, 01:00–26 Oct, 00:59, inc

* Subtract two hours from the birth time to convert it to GMT.

Annual Sun Sign Changes

If your birthday falls within these dates and times, you are an Aquarian. If you were born in January before the first date and time, you are a Capricorn. If you were born in February after the second date and time, you are a Piscean. All times are given in GMT, using the 24-hour clock.

1920 21 Jan, 08:05–19 Feb, 22:28 inc　**1948** 21 Jan, 03:19–19 Feb, 17:36 inc
1921 20 Jan, 13:55–19 Feb, 04:19 inc　**1949** 20 Jan, 09:09–18 Feb, 23:27 inc
1922 20 Jan, 19:48–19 Feb, 10:16 inc　**1950** 20 Jan, 15:00–19 Feb, 05:17 inc
1923 21 Jan, 01:35–19 Feb, 15:59 inc　**1951** 20 Jan, 20:53–19 Feb, 11:09 inc
1924 21 Jan, 07:29–19 Feb, 21:51 inc　**1952** 21 Jan, 02:39–19 Feb, 16:56 inc
1925 20 Jan, 13:21–19 Feb, 03:42 inc　**1953** 20 Jan, 08:22–18 Feb, 22:41 inc
1926 20 Jan, 19:13–19 Feb, 09:34 inc　**1954** 20 Jan, 14:12–19 Feb, 04:32 inc
1927 21 Jan, 01:12–19 Feb, 15:34 inc　**1955** 20 Jan, 20:02–19 Feb, 10:18 inc
1928 21 Jan, 06:57–19 Feb, 21:19 inc　**1956** 21 Jan, 01:49–19 Feb, 16:04 inc
1929 20 Jan, 12:43–19 Feb, 03:06 inc　**1957** 20 Jan, 07:39–18 Feb, 21:58 inc
1930 20 Jan, 18:33–19 Feb, 08:59 inc　**1958** 20 Jan, 13:29–19 Feb, 03:48 inc
1931 21 Jan, 00:18–19 Feb, 14:40 inc　**1959** 20 Jan, 19:19–19 Feb, 09:37 inc
1932 20 Jan, 06:07–19 Feb, 20:28 inc　**1960** 21 Jan, 01:11–19 Feb, 15:26 inc
1933 20 Jan, 11:53–19 Feb, 02:16 inc　**1961** 20 Jan, 07:02–18 Feb, 21:16 inc
1934 20 Jan, 17:37–19 Feb, 08:01 inc　**1962** 20 Jan, 12:58–19 Feb, 03:14 inc
1935 20 Jan, 23:29–19 Feb, 13:51 inc　**1963** 20 Jan, 18:54–19 Feb, 09:08 inc
1936 20 Jan, 05:13–19 Feb, 19:32 inc　**1964** 21 Jan, 00:42–19 Feb, 14:57 inc
1937 20 Jan, 11:01–19 Feb, 01:20 inc　**1965** 20 Jan, 06:29–18 Feb, 20:47 inc
1938 20 Jan, 16:59–19 Feb, 07:19 inc　**1966** 20 Jan, 12:20–19 Feb, 02:37 inc
1939 20 Jan, 22:51–19 Feb, 13:09 inc　**1967** 20 Jan, 18:08–19 Feb, 08:23 inc
1940 21 Jan, 04:45–19 Feb, 19:03 inc　**1968** 20 Jan, 23:55–19 Feb, 14:09 inc
1941 20 Jan, 10:34–19 Feb, 00:56 inc　**1969** 20 Jan, 05:39–18 Feb, 19:54 inc
1942 20 Jan, 16:24–19 Feb, 06:46 inc　**1970** 20 Jan, 11:24–19 Feb, 01:41 inc
1943 20 Jan, 22:19–19 Feb, 12:40 inc　**1971** 20 Jan, 17:13–19 Feb, 07:27 inc
1944 21 Jan, 04:08–19 Feb, 18:27 inc　**1972** 20 Jan, 23:00–19 Feb, 13:11 inc
1945 20 Jan, 09:54–19 Feb, 00:14 inc　**1973** 20 Jan, 04:49–18 Feb, 19:01 inc
1946 20 Jan, 15:45–19 Feb, 06:08 inc　**1974** 20 Jan, 10:46–19 Feb, 00:58 inc
1947 20 Jan, 21:32–19 Feb, 11:51 inc　**1975** 20 Jan, 16:37–19 Feb, 06:49 inc

1976 20 Jan, 22:26–19 Feb, 12:40 inc
1977 20 Jan, 04:15–18 Feb, 18:30 inc
1978 20 Jan, 10:05–19 Feb, 00:21 inc
1979 20 Jan, 16:01–19 Feb, 06:13 inc
1980 20 Jan, 21:49–19 Feb, 12:02 inc
1981 20 Jan, 03:37–18 Feb, 17:52 inc
1982 20 Jan, 09:32–18 Feb, 23:46 inc
1983 20 Jan, 15:18–19 Feb, 05:30 inc
1984 20 Jan, 21:06–19 Feb, 11:16 inc
1985 20 Jan, 02:58–18 Feb, 17:07 inc
1986 20 Jan, 08:47–18 Feb, 22:57 inc
1987 20 Jan, 14:41–19 Feb, 04:50 inc
1988 20 Jan, 20:25–19 Feb, 10:35 inc
1989 20 Jan, 02:08–18 Feb, 16:20 inc

1990 20 Jan, 08:03–18 Feb, 22:14 inc
1991 20 Jan, 13:48–19 Feb, 03:58 inc
1992 20 Jan, 19:33–19 Feb, 09:43 inc
1993 20 Jan, 01:24–18 Feb, 15:35 inc
1994 20 Jan, 07:08–18 Feb, 21:22 inc
1995 20 Jan, 13:01–19 Feb, 03:11 inc
1996 20 Jan, 18:54–19 Feb, 09:01 inc
1997 20 Jan, 00:44–18 Feb, 14:52 inc
1998 20 Jan, 06:47–18 Feb, 20:55 inc
1999 20 Jan, 12:38–19 Feb, 02:47 inc
2000 20 Jan, 18:24–19 Feb, 08:33 inc
2001 20 Jan, 00:17–18 Feb, 14:27 inc
2002 20 Jan, 06:03–18 Feb, 20:13 inc
2003 20 Jan, 11:54–19 Feb, 02:00 inc